Dark Fairies

By Dr. Bob Curran

Illustrated by Ian Daniels

New Page Books
A Division of The Career Press, Inc.
Pompton Plains, N.J.

Dark Fairies
Edited and Typeset by Gina Hoogerhyde
Cover design by Michael Pye and Jeff Piasky
Cover art by Ian Daniels
Printed in the U.S.A. by Courier

To order this title, please call toll-free 1-800-CAREER-1 (NJ and Canada: 201-848-0310) to order using VISA or MasterCard, or for further information on books from Career Press.

The Career Press, Inc., 220 West Parkway, Unit 12
Pompton Plains, NJ 07444
www.careerpress.com
www.newpagebooks.com

Library of Congress Cataloging-in-Publication Data

Curran, Bob.
    Dark fairies / by Bob Curran.
        p. cm.
    Includes index.
    ISBN 978-1-60163-110-7 (pbk) -- ISBN 978-1-60163-726-0
    (e-book) 1. Fairies. I
    Title.

BF1552.C87 2010
398' .45--dc22

                                       2009051734

Contents

Introduction: The Good People?
5

Chapter 1: The People of the Mounds
23

Chapter 2: The Host of the Air
59

Chapter 3: The Dwellers in the Depths
91

Chapter 4: Away With the Fairies
125

Conclusion: The Other Sort
175

Bibliography
183

Index
187

About the Author
191

Introduction

The Good People?

alt Disney has a lot to answer for. Arguably it is he, among others, who has formed our impression of fairies, through his characterization of Tinkerbell, as frail, flickering beings who flitter about on gossamer wings doing good as they go. In the Celtic world, we have the idea of jolly elves and leprechauns, whose activities mirror those of human society: they get drunk and try to cheat each other—though in a good-natured way—and fight with each other. Such an image has been made famous by the likes of Robert Stevenson's 1959 Disney Studios film *Darby O'Gill and the Little People,* which in turn was based on Herminie Templeton-Kavanagh's book *Darby O'Gill and the Good People,* originally published as a series of episodes in *McClure's Magazine* between 1901 and 1902 . (Although born in County Longford, Ireland, Templeton-Kavanagh was the wife of Marcus Kavanagh, an American judge, and spent much of her life in Cook County, Chicago, Illinois.) This portrayed the fairies as living a sort of idyllic, easy-going, stage-Irish lifestyle in a sort of rural village environment, either helping humans or playing harmless pranks on them when it fancied them. Because of her Irish ancestry and because her ideas (as portrayed by Disney) fit in well with a kind of "stock Irishness" (which actually bore little resemblance to rural Ireland) current in America at the time, the notion of such fairies became deeply ingrained in the public psyche and, thus, the idea of luminous flittering creatures or roguish goblins were seen as an actual part of folklore as far as many people were concerned. It was (and to some extent still is) taken to mean a species of supernatural creatures that are essentially benign, and to all intents and purposes, either shy of or friendly toward humans; this concept has continued down even until today. We speak of the Tooth Fairy (a generous being who leaves financial reward for the lost teeth of children) or of a Fairy Godmother (a beneficent creature who watches over us, shields us from harm, and ensures that we enjoy largely unwarranted good fortune). Both of these figures contain the underlying cultural motif of a benign supernatural race existing somewhere alongside ourselves. But just how true is such a perception? It is probably not that accurate at all.

The word *fairy* is said to have originated in medieval times (possibly the 12th or 13th centuries); its root word *fay* or *fae* was sometimes taken to mean "spirit-touched." The exact origin of the word is probably older and dates back to early medieval or even Roman times. It might have its roots in the Latin word *fatui*, which referred mainly to gasses—usually a mixture of methane and phosphates, which were seen hovering above swamps, the edges of lakes, cemeteries, or boggy places. The word is still in use in the term *ignis fatui* (flammable marsh gas). These gasses may have been the origins of a belief in will-o-the-wisps.

Fatui

For early man such gaseous activity was interpreted not as a natural phenomena, but as the involvement of the spirit world; such interpretations gave rise to a belief in a race of almost invisible beings—the *Fatui*—that lived in such places. The Fatui were generally considered to be malignant and hostile toward human beings, luring them into their own dangerous environments or muddling their minds so much that they did not know where they were or what they were doing (the source of our word *infatuation*). These bursts of fiery gasses were often accorded supernatural powers in their own right—they were the spirits of the marsh or of the graveyard, and had probably existed there since the world began. By the later medieval period the word seems to have become *fay*, which had a slightly wider connotation in that it was suggestive of interaction between this spirit race and Humankind. Such interaction may have occurred for a couple of reasons: one, inadvertently, or two, for the acquisition of supernatural powers for the individual concerned.

Morgan Le Fay

Arguably the most celebrated of these people was Morgan le Fay, half-sister to King Arthur and a prevalent character in Arthurian romance. It is with her that, according to some sources, the King was said to have enjoyed an incestuous relationship, eventually giving birth to Mordred, who would finally and fatally wound Arthur at the Battle of Camlann. According to other sources, Mordred is the son of her sister Morgause, who was, in some texts, another semi-supernatural creature. In all traditions, however, it is clear the Morgan is not altogether human—hence her nickname "le Fay" (or "le fey" or "le fee"), meaning "of the fairy." Through this supernatural connection, she would come to be recognized as the greatest enchantress of Arthurian legend. And yet, in her original incarnation, she remained essentially human. She was, in fact, human enough to cause the great wizard Merlin to lust after her (in some variants of the legend she is his mistress and he taught her magic), or to be briefly married to a human king. In later legend, however, she became a "Queen of the Faerie," a supernatural creature in her own right, commanding mystical powers and without many human attributes. She had become a true "woman of the fairy" and her powers were perceived to come from her contact with Otherworldly forces.

Tam Lin

Morgan was, of course, not the only human to have been "spirit-touched." The hero of Tam Lin (also Tamline or Tam-a-line), an old ballad from the Border Region of Scotland, has many similar attributes. According to the legend that forms the basis of the ballad, Tam was a fairy/human figure who lived in Carterhaugh Wood near Selkirk, who extracted a toll from those who passed through it. From men, he demanded money, but when a virgin passed through the woods, he demanded her virginity as payment. According to some variations, Tam had once been a human knight who, while passing through the Wood, had been thrown by his horse and killed. He had, however, been brought back to life by the forces of nature inherent in the landscape all around (as exemplified in the form of a single entity given as

"the Faerie Queen" or "Queen of Elfland"), and was now something slightly more than human. The legend continues that the lord's daughter, whose name is sometimes given as either Margaret or Janet, went to the Wood to pick roses and was accosted by Tam, who demanded the usual payment. On returning home, the girl found that she was pregnant; fearing that she would not be able to get a husband the girl decided to rid herself of the child. She visited an elderly monk who told her of a certain herb that grew in Carterhaugh Wood, which if taken would induce a miscarriage. She went once more to the Wood, but as she was gathering the herb, Tam reappeared in great anger and forbade her to do so. He explained that he had once been human, and although he could never become so again, he desired human offspring, which is why he demanded the virginity of any maiden who trespassed in the Wood. There was also a certain urgency to the situation. Every seven years the fairies paid a tribute to Hell (in the legend they were said to be the offspring of Hell) by giving one of their own to the Devil, and Tam feared that he would be next. The girl promised to help him if he would act as a father to her baby, and he promised that he would. He was to ride among a number of fairy knights through Carterhaugh Wood and the girl was to wait, concealed, until he passed. Then she was to jump out and drag him away before the others could stop her. As long as she held onto him, they could not retrieve him; however, they tried to turn him into all different horrible things in order to make her drop him; if he touched the ground, the fairies would have power over him once more. She ran for a certain holy well near the center of the Wood, and when he turned into a burning coal, she threw him into the sacred waters. He appeared before her as a naked man and the fairies' power over him broke. The fairies were not pleased, and showed their displeasure by creating storms and poor harvests around the border areas, but all the same they honored the bargain. It is unclear as to whether Tam actually became human again, but he appears to have lived the rest of his life as an ordinary man (although some version still attributed certain subsequent supernatural powers to him). The basic legend was used as the source for a number of ballads sung around the border region, several of which were collected by James Francis Child, the noted American folksong collector, and appears in his collection known as *The Child Ballads*. The story is not unique to the Scottish borders (though this version is perhaps the best known), but variants of it, under a variety of names, appear in other traditions, for example in Brittany (France) and Germany. And, in an even wider sense, Tam Lin remains among a number of other such humans who have had connections with the "fairy" kind with varying results.

Religious Beliefs

Similar to those who were led astray by or associated with the Fatui, Tam seemed to receive his power from the natural world around him—in this case the forces that resided in Carterhaugh Wood. This led to a common perception that fairies were perhaps no more than the embodiment of forces that dwelt within the landscape of a particular area, and maybe even the environment in its entirety. This was particularly true in Celtic belief, which invested such natural things as rivers, trees, wells, and rocks with some kind of supernatural intelligence and awareness. In fact, the ramshackle religion of the Western Celts often venerated these forces, with their priests worshipping at great stones, groves of trees, or at rivers, waterfalls, and pools. Indeed, such forces were often considered to be extremely hostile toward frail Humankind, and not to offer such worship was to invite their wrath—whether it be in the form of poor harvests or in the shape of natural disasters, such as floods or droughts. In time such forces became equated with the idea of Pagan gods (the remnants of old worship); this fact is often given as a possible origin of the fairy belief: that they were, in fact, antique, Pagan nature deities by another name. As Christianity began to expand in the Western world, such an explanation became more common. They were accredited with powers such as those possessed by ancient gods, and in many respects needed to be placated, just as the former gods themselves had been. And, like the deities, they could be extremely capricious and hostile toward humans who lived within their specific areas. Similar to the gods themselves, they could bring ill fortune on an individual or on a community, and, other than placating them and treating them with extreme respect, it was usually best to avoid them altogether.

In the Christian world, alongside this belief in ancient Pagan gods, was a concomitant theory that fairies might indeed be fallen angels. This merged Christian tradition with more ancient beliefs, and placed the fairies within a recognizable religious framework. There was a legend, prevalent in some parts of the Western Christian world, that when Lucifer and his minions had risen up in rebellion against God prior to the foundation of the world, a number of angels had "sat on the fence," unwilling to take either side. When God triumphed and Lucifer was cast into the fiery pit (to become the Devil), God came to judge these indifferent angels. They were judged as not being evil enough to be consigned to Hell with Lucifer, but not righteous enough to be accepted back into Heaven. Therefore, a middle ground was found for them, and they were "cast down" onto the earth where they became the fairy kind. However, they still retained at least some of their former angelic powers (and also hostility toward humans with whom they shared the world). It was believed that some angels were jealous of humans, who were, after all, God's supreme and favored creation. As they continued to dwell on earth—some on the land, some in the air, some in the seas—they saw how God looked after Mankind and allowed humans to prosper; this increased their antipathy toward the human race, making them even more dangerous as time went on.

The Fairie Race

During the 13th and 14th centuries another idea as to the origin of fairies began to emerge—especially in some Celtic countries—which was more logical and slightly less superstitious in tone. This was the supposition that fairies were the last remnants of a prehistoric race (or of a number of prehistoric races) that had been defeated by incoming invaders and forced into hiding among the countryside. The notion of such invasions is the central theme of a loose collection of Irish texts—the *Lebor Gabala Erenn* (the *Book of Invasions* or the *Book of the Taking of Ireland)*, compiled and edited by an unknown scribe somewhere around the 11th century. This is a mixture of legend, pseudohistory, and actual historical fact, and details a number of invasions of Ireland that are alleged to have occurred in prehistoric times. Among the invaders who arrived in the country were the Tuatha de

Danann (the Children of the Goddess Danu), who are said to have come from the East in a golden cloud. These individuals were small and golden-skinned, with great learning and understanding of the world around them. They were wonderworkers and highly skilled in magic arts, but were ultimately defeated and driven out of the country by the war-like Milesians, who were the ancestors of the Gaels. Those of them who remained—concealed from human eyes—became the ancestors of the fairies. Many still kept their own powers and skills, which the Milesians (and subsequently the Gaels from whom the Irish are descended) did not have.

The belief may have had some merit, for, when the Celts arrived in the West after being driven out of the Po Valley in Italy by the expanding Roman Empire, they may well have dislodged a number of older, aboriginal races that retreated into the forests, bogs, and mountains to escape. Underground dwellings sometimes discovered to have belonged to former peoples, were attributed to the fairy folk; ancient tools and burial ornamentation that were sometimes found in mounds and hillocks were likewise attributed.

However, there was also a supernatural aspect to the belief. In some variants, the Tuatha de Danann had not hidden themselves away in remote and inaccessible places, but had withdrawn into a mystic Otherworld which lay somewhere beyond mortal vision. Descriptions of this Otherworld—a central tenet of Celtic belief—were exceptionally vague. Sometimes it was described as an actual country that coexisted with the human world, which allowed the beings there to cross over; at others it was said to be an island that lay well out to sea in the West, which appeared in the mortal world once every seven years. The island was known under various names, one of which was Hy Brasail, where Brasail, the Celtic King of the World, held court. In some other variations it was Emhain Alba (the Fort of Apples) that is rendered in English and Arthurian traditions as "The Fortunate Isle" where Morgan le Fay ruled. This is where the dying Arthur was taken after the Battle of Camlann, and where he is said to rest, awaiting the call when Britain needs him again to defend her shores. This was supposed to be an earthly paradise and a home to the fairy kind; similar to Hy Brasail it lay somewhere "away in the West" (the descriptions of its location are extremely vague). Some legends said that it was where the sun went down. The Fortunate Isle (or Isles) was also a place to which the "blessed dead" (like King Arthur) traveled when their time on Earth was over and where they continued to live in idyllic happiness, fully aware of what went on within the mortal realm. This idea led to another intriguing and extremely popular speculation concerning the exact nature of fairies.

Fairies and the Dead

It was thought that fairies might indeed be the souls of the dead, returning to the human world in some sort of spirit form, or that they might be some subclass of the dead. Such an idea may have sprung from the belief that fairies were in some way connected with ancient mounds and tumuli dotted throughout the Celtic countryside, and these were, in fact, the burial places of dead warriors or chieftains. In some parts of the Celtic world—England, Brittany, and Wales—it was considered ill or unlucky to eat food that had grown in such places (wild berries and such), because this was often referred to as "fairy food," and the dead (or the fairies) would take revenge on those who consumed it. In some tales in popular Irish and Scottish cultures the terms *ghost* and *fairy* were often interchangeable, as were ghost and fairy stories. In the north of England, for example, the word *barguest* (or *bargest*) is suggestive of a type of invisible fairy who creates mischief (it sometimes takes the shape of a dog or demonic hound), and it can also mean a type of ghost or spirit, usually of an evil person. One of the most famous northern fairy stories—*The Cauld Lad of Hylton* (who is often portrayed as an elf)—is actually a ghost story.

Baron Hylton

The area of Hylton, close to Sutherland on the Scottish Borders, was at one time owned by the Hylton family; in the late 17th century it was the property of Robert Hylton, the 13th Baron Hylton. He is said to have had a beautiful daughter who was courted by a stable boy, Robert Skelton. Finding the two of them *in flagrante*, the baron lost his temper and attacked Skelton. Here there are variations in the tale as to what he did. In one version, he decapitated Skelton; in another he ran him through with a pitchfork; in a third, he battered him until he broke his skull. Whatever occurred, Robert Skelton was dead. In fact, the baron stood trial for the murder, but was able to produce an alibi, although it is widely suggested that he paid for it. An old man told the court that he had asked Skelton to fetch something from a high shelf in one of the stables and that the boy had fallen and killed himself. Baron Hylton, he said, had actually tended the boy's injuries. The baron was formally pardoned in 1609. However, shortly after Skelton's death, strange things began to happen at Hylton Castle, which might be consistent with poltergeist activity. Things were moved about and inexplicably broken; pots (including chamber pots) were emptied and potatoes were thrown about by their own volition. Odd sounds, such as a voice crying, were sometimes heard in the castle at night, and this was said to be fairy activity coming from a nearby site that was reputedly fairy-haunted. According to the legend, a cook decided to sit up one night in order to see what was causing the disturbance. Around midnight, a naked boy appeared, who resembled the unfortunate Skelton, weeping and crying "I'm cauld (cold)! I'm cauld!" The cook, showing no fear, immediately rose and put a cloak about the apparition's shoulders. It is here that the story varies; in some versions this finally put an end to the supernatural activity, but in others, the disturbances continued, albeit less frequently. There was even a poem that was associated with the spirit, which was allegedly spoken as it vanished.

Here's a cloak an' here's a hood,
The Cauld Lad of Hylton will do nae more good.

This, of course, is little more than a piece of doggerel, which has been added at some later date in order to bolster the story. The tale of the Cauld Lad has more of the qualities of a ghost story than of a fairy legend, and yet the spirit seems to have been more closely associated with elves and gnomes than with a spectre. The apparition was said to be that of a bargest (barghast, barguest, or barguiest), a fairy creature common in parts of Cumberland and Durham in the north of England. This fairy spirit could take various forms. It could be invisible and act like a poltergeist, or, more commonly, it could take the form of a great hound that dripped fire and sparks from its jaws. It could also take the form of a little spectral man, who flitted from room to room in certain houses like a phantom. Indeed, it was sometimes referred to as "the house elf," although the name is thought to have come from the German *berg geist* meaning "mountain spirit." Others argue that its origins may lie in "*buhr-geist*" meaning a "town ghost." In both cases, the word *geist* appears, denoting a spirit of the dead, although the word refers to a fairy (or sometimes demon) who is hostile toward Mankind.

Today, Hylton Castle is no more than a picturesque ruin, although locals state that the cries of the Cauld Lad can still be heard echoing from it, and a sinister presence can be felt by many who venture there.

Irish Encounters

Connections between fairies and the dead extend beyond the north of England and the borders of Scotland. In Ireland and Wales there are stories of people who have encountered the fairy kind, and who have remarked upon their resemblance to dead friends or family. Near Claremorris, County Mayo, in the Republic of Ireland, during the late 1800s, a man walking home from a sheeben (illegal drinking house) passed by a great house close to the road where there seemed to be a party in progress. The house seemed to be lit up with laughter, music, and people. This, he surmised, was a fairy house, and he knew that some of the fairies in this region were extremely hospitable and that he might receive more drink. He stepped in the great door and saw that the guests were all dancing to the strains of wonderful music, but as the dancers whirled past him, he saw that every one of them had the face of a long-dead neighbor. The vision both sobered and horrified him.

"In the Name of God!" he cried out in terror. At that moment there was a clap of thunder and the entire company vanished away. He stood in a ruin with the wind blowing and the rain lashing down. All traces of the dead/fairy kind had gone as if they had never existed at the sound of the holy name. The man returned home in a shocked state and went to Mass the following morning in order to rid himself of any residual fairy magic, for he considered that the encounter could damn his immortal soul.

Again, a kind of poltergeist activity occurred in the vicinity of a fairy rath (ancient earthworks attributed to the fairy kind) near Larne in County Antrim during the early 1700s. Passersby were pelted with stones from the rath, which were said to be thrown by hostile fairies, and a number of alarming events happened in a nearby rectory. Here, an old woman—the mother-in-law of the incumbent clergyman—was tormented by frightening visions, and was almost overcome by noxious smells reputedly caused by invisible beings that were described as fairies. The exorcism of a clergyman was called upon, but this only seems to have had a limited effect. The "fairies" in the fort were adjudged to be the hostile spirits of the dead who tormented and attacked the local populace, including a minister of religion.

Banshees

One of the most famous of all Irish fairies—the banshee—is sometimes also believed to be some kind of ghost. Her name means "woman of the fairy," but her appearance is often described as being that of a drifting, wailing spirit. She is supposed to follow some of the great families of Ireland—at one time it was only said to be families with either "O'" or "Mac" in their names, denoting a long, Gaelic ancestry, but often the belief extends more widely than that—unerringly predicting when prominent members would die. In some accounts, she was believed to be an ancestral figure of someone long dead and belonging to the family itself. This placed her well within the realms of ghosts or phantoms, and often created a quandary as to her exact nature—was she, for example, a ghost or a fairy? Perhaps both, with the notion stemming from the idea that the dead and the fairies are in fact the same thing.

Emotions

Another belief concerning the Good Folk (as fairies were called in some cultures), was that they were beings created independently of angels, humans, or the dead. This made them elemental beings, and it was said they might even be created out of the stuff of human emotion. For instance, an angry word might take on some form of substance and become one of the evil fairy kind, while a good thought might create a beneficent ethereal creature. Therefore, a fierce argument might generate a host of beings, all of whom were inimical to Mankind. The idea, which was common during the 19th century, was taken up by the writer J.M. Barrie, the famous creator of Peter Pan. In his 1902 novel *The Little White Bird*, Barrie suggested that the first laugh of a baby was incredibly precious, and as soon as it came into contact with the air, it shattered into a thousand pieces, each one a fairy, and this was the real origin of the fairy race. This romanticized but rather sweet view of things was a firm belief among many rural English folk into the early 20th century. The same was said, however, about words that were uttered in spite or envy by grown people. The moral implication here is, of course, rather obvious.

Elements

Of course, fairies might be created not from words or laughter, but from natural elements and conditions. They might be created, for example, by a coalition of mists along a riverbank, or they might emerge out of the rotting bark of a tree that has fallen in the forest. They could even emerge from the mold or dirt in the corner of a house. Their disposition was sometimes said to depend upon their point of origin—for instance, those who emerged from rot, dirt, rust, or mold were considered to be extremely sly and rather bad tempered. Those that had emerged out of the mist or fog were considered to be more mellow or else indifferent toward humans. Other such elemental entities might have been no more than the embodiment of trees, plants, rocks, or water, and these were considered to be forms of fairies nonetheless.

Demons

Yet another interpretation of the fairy kind in Western Christendom was that they were demons. As the old Pagan spirits of house and countryside began to wither away before the advancing light of Christianity they began to change into things of abject evil. They were, argued certain clerics, the agents of the Evil One himself and were obliged to do his bidding by leading the faithful away from righteousness. Fairies and their like were to be avoided at all costs; at least, that is what the Church taught. They were tempters and murderers and might lure the unwary into ways they did not want to go, thus damning his or her immortal soul forever. Fairies, in fact, were the imps of Hell—after all, did they not live somewhere underground, which was the dominion of Satan? Dealing with them was just as bad as dealing with the Devil, and it held the same consequences, for the fairies were tricky and sly and rejoiced in nothing more than a human soul that was lost to God.

And in some traditions, such as in the Western Isles of Scotland and parts of Ireland, some fairies are so evil as to be equated with vampires, drinking blood from humankind in order to sustain themselves. In parts of Mayo and Cavan, as well as in places such as Benbecula and South Uist, they took blood in order to keep themselves alive and to give themselves strength, either for fighting each other or for hurling competitions. In many areas, too, fairies were renowned for stealing very young babies before they were baptized and carrying them off into some bleak otherworld (a demon land), leaving perhaps a changeling in its place. The notion of changelings and stolen children will be examined later in this book. It was necessary for humans to protect small children by marking them as either human or Christian. This entailed placing them under a crucifix or throwing an item of human clothing across their bed. I myself, who have never been baptized, was raised in an area where this belief was very strong. My grandfather threw his coat over the place where I was lying as I slept to mark me as a human child. (It was widely believed at that time that fairies would steal infants away when they slept). For my own neighbors, fairies were considered to be particularly evil and dangerous.

Fairies, then, are not the flittering, flimsy, good-hearted creatures of a Walt Disney film. Neither are they the jolly little artisans who mischievously play generally harmless pranks on unsuspecting humans. They are something much different and sometimes far more sinister. They were the last vestiges of ancient gods, the remnants of a hostile aboriginal race, the unquiet dead; elemental beings composed out of the very things that make up Humankind, including human emotions; or, perhaps they are demons seeking to lure God's chosen to the very doors of Hell. Whatever fairies were, our ancestors felt that they had good reason to fear them. Come now as we explore that not-so-comfortable world of the fairy folk, a world that lies within the borders of genuine folklore and tradition, and where very little might be as it initially appears. One thing's for sure; if you enjoy the fairytale films of Walt Disney it will probably not be what you expect.

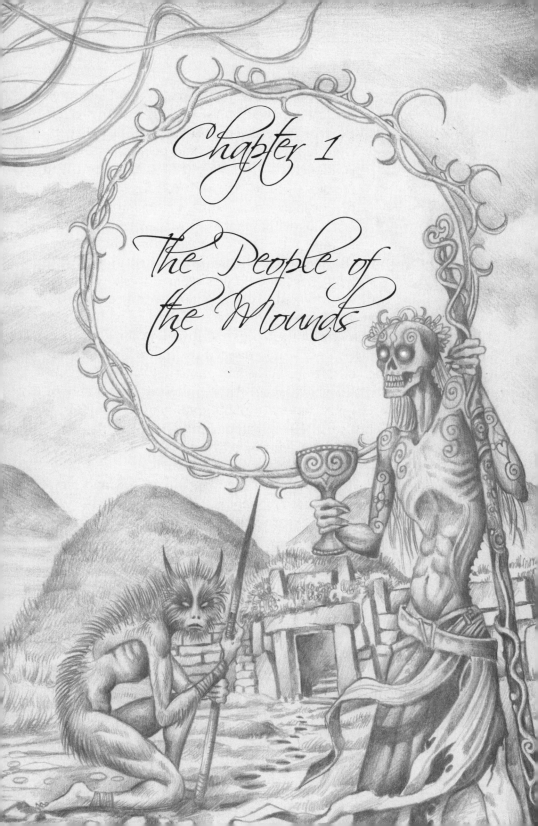

Chapter 1

The People of
the Mounds

I n the year 1920, with the Great War not long over, the leading Theosophist Edward L. Gardener unexpectedly received two photographs that excited him greatly. They had been taken by two young girls—Elsie Wright, 16, and her friend Frances Griffiths, 10, both cousins in the village of Cottingley near Bingley, Yorkshire, England, using an old Butcher Midg Magazine camera that belonged to Elsie's father. What the pictures showed was truly amazing. Taken in 1917, the badly developed prints seemed to show Frances Griffiths playing with what looked like tiny people with gossamer-like wings—the traditional children's book image of the fairies. Both girls claimed that they had met with the fairies in Cottingley Glen (Cottingley Beck) and that the little people had danced for them. Elsie's father, Arthur, was extremely suspicious of the first photo of Frances surrounded by dancing fairies, and when the girls later produced a second photo, he forbade Elsie to use his camera to photograph fairies again. Elsie's mother, Polly, was not so sure. She had embraced some of the teachings of Theosophy and was more inclined to believe in the existence of supernatural beings than her more skeptical husband.

Theosophy was a combination of religious philosophy and metaphysics that had originated with Madam H.P. Blavatsky (1831–1896). Its central tenet was that the Great Soul of the Universe sought to help Mankind through various means—including major world religions; sometimes by very esoteric practices. This had given rise to Spiritual Hierarchy, a number of mahatmas or leaders living in a remote area of Tibet with whom Madam Blavatsky was in direct contact through supernatural means. Although it is not clear if Polly Wright fully believed in Theosophy, she probably believed enough to accept the existence of supernatural beings such as fairies, and she believed her daughter. It was she who sent the photos to Gardener for his opinion in 1920.

The quality of the prints that Polly Wright had sent were relatively poor (they had been taken more than three years before and not by an expert hand), and they seemed faded, so Gardener sent them to a photographer friend, Harold Snelling, to see if he could enhance them and produce prints that were of sufficient quality to prove their authenticity. Gardener was now convinced that the photographs were genuine. Snelling did a more-than-adequate job in reprinting the photos, and his images are still in use to this day. They show Francis in the background with a troop of Tinkerbell-like fairies dancing in front of her on some tree branches. These were the images that had alarmed the dubious Mr. Wright when he (a keen amateur photographer) had developed the film. However, both Elsie and Francis were adamant that they had met the fairies in the Glen and that they were the trooping spirits of the countryside. The fairies were kind and gentle and very much like those that they read about in their children's books. The photographs were sent for analysis, and although a number of photographers passed them as genuine, the laboratories at Kodak photography—the major U.K. photographic company of the time—refused to authenticate them.

Perhaps the affair of the Cottingley fairies would simply have re-mained as a curious footnote had it not been for the involvement of a particular individual. Sir Arthur Conan Doyle, the creator of the legendary fictional detective Sherlock Holmes, was a friend of Gardener and also a well-known Spiritualist of the time. As such he was a firm believer in supernatural beings. In 1920 as a regular contributor to the publication, he had been asked by *The Strand Magazine* to write an article on fairies for its Christmas edition. Around this time, Gardener passed him the photographs, which had been taken in Cottingley. Doyle was convinced that they were genuine, but passed them to a renowned psychical researcher, Sir Oliver Lodge, who suggested that they might be fakes. He thought that perhaps Arthur Wright, who was a skilled photographer and had often experimented with new techniques, had somehow managed to transpose a picture of a troupe of costumed dancers onto the photograph in order to back up his daughter's claim. Conan Doyle, however, was still convinced that they were genuine and that they were spirits of the landscape, just as the girls had claimed. He arranged for the prints of the photographs that had been enhanced by Snelling to be published in *The Strand* where they were greeted with astounded interest. However, the common consensus was as before: they were traditional dancers who had been somehow superimposed onto the plate containing the image of Frances Griffiths, perhaps by Arthur Wright. It was also known that during World War I, Elsie had worked in a local photographic studios preparing photos of fallen soldiers for loved ones from plates, and she may have had some knowledge of the superimposition process.

Gardener suggested that if the children were well connected to the fairies then further photographs might be taken, which would settle the matter once and for all. He especially wanted to take a picture of one of them flying with its gossamer wings. The photo shoot was arranged during the school holidays in August 1920 when both girls would be available. Frances Griffiths traveled up to Cottingley from Scarborough where she had gone to live with her parents after the First World War while Edward Gardener traveled from London to Bradford and then on to Cottingley. With him he brought two dozen secretly marked photographic plates.

The experiment lasted from Thursday until Saturday with the girls calling the fairies and with Gardener ready to photograph whatever appeared. They took several photographs but none of any note except one that showed an ill-defined figure that nobody could make out. It certainly bore no resemblance to anything in the previous photographs, and Gardener was not sure if it wasn't some sort of natural phenomena. Conan Doyle, however, remained convinced, and in 1922 he published a book entitled *The Coming of the Fairies*, which included a photograph (supposedly taken in 1920) showing Frances with a fairy seated on the branch of a tree beside her. This is often judged to be the clearest photo yet, and although it showed the fairy clad in traditional garb, there were suggestions of a rather substantial body beneath the clothes. Moreover, both Conan Doyle and Gardener attempted to contact the fairies by holding several séances, none of which were successful.

Although interest in the Cottingley fairies remained high among Spiritualists, the girls themselves had begun to grow weary of all the attention. They were growing much older anyway—too old for fairies. Probably the final straw came in August 1921 when the noted clairvoyant Geoffrey Hodson traveled to Cottingley in an attempt to contact the fairies. There were no photographs taken this time, although Hodson claimed to have seen the good people (although he later admitted that he was guided by Elsie). Much later, both Elsie and Frances admitted that they had tricked Hodson in order to make him appear foolish. It seemed that they had a somewhat malicious attitude toward many of those who believed in them. They wanted little to do with the whole business, refusing all interviews until much later.

In fact, after a period at Bradford Art College (where she studied, among other things, photography), Elsie emigrated to the United States after marrying a local engineer. She was to stay there throughout World War II, only returning to England in 1947 at the end of hostilities. Frances continued to live with her parents in Cottingley for a time before marrying a soldier, Sidney Way, and moving to Ramsgate in 1928. They very seldom spoke about the fairy episode. When they did, it was to assent that the photographs were in fact genuine and that the fairies in them had been the embodiments of nature.

However, in 1981 both women were interviewed for *Unexplained Magazine* by the writer Joe Cooper. Frances continued to maintain that they had indeed met the fairies and continued to do so until her death in 1986; Elsie (who died in 1988), however, admitted that they had been faked. They had carefully cut out drawings of fairies from books and had placed them on hat pins, so that they could be photographed. She went on to say that she had been too embarrassed to admit to it at the time because of Sir Arthur Conan Doyle's involvement. She hadn't liked to contradict such a great man. (In this statement she said more than her father, Arthur, who publicly derided Conan Doyle at the time, saying that it was strange how such an educated man could be taken in by a girl who had been bottom of her class in school.) But she would later partially retract her statement (perhaps in the face of some adverse reaction) and state that the photograph used in Conan Doyle's book was in fact genuine. This was the position she maintained until her death, but by now many people were highly skeptical. In a final twist to the story, the original photos showed up again in January 2009 during the filming of the popular BBC Television program *Antiques Roadshow* in Belfast when Frances Way's (formerly Griffiths) daughter and granddaughter brought the plates in to be valued. Both of them were asked in front of television cameras as to whether the photographs were genuine, and both were convinced of their authenticity.

Despite Elsie Wright's confession, the affair of the Cottingley fairies has continued to fascinate and intrigue many throughout the years, perhaps because of Conan Doyle's involvement, or because it appeals to a desire in all of us for the photographs to really be genuine, and for there truly to be good little people lurking out there among the foliage. But how true was the girls' assessment (and the assessment of others) that those creatures they "saw" were indeed the spirits of nature, that they were benign and willing to reveal themselves to humans? For many centuries—long before Elsie and Frances went down to the Cottingley Glen—people have believed that someone or *something* lurked out there in the hills and woodlands of the countryside, just beyond the line of human sight.

Tree Fairies

In ancient Greek mythology, for example, many clusters of trees and woodlands were said to be haunted by nature spirits known as dryads. The name came from the ancient Greek *drys* meaning oak, although the root word is older—*derew*—an extremely ancient Indo-European word meaning "tree." These were, in fact, the embodiments of the trees themselves and were probably the remnants of ancient vegetative gods, which had been worshipped since earliest times. They were also perhaps the forerunners of what the Cottingley fairies were perceived to be. However, the Greeks were not alone in believing that trees were inhabited by such beings, for the idea of men living in the trees and the woodland undergrowth appears in the mythologies and cultures of a number of ancient peoples.

Although the dryads and similar beings are generally portrayed as placid creatures, living and dying with the individual growths with which they were associated, this was not necessarily the case. In many ancient cultures these creatures actually *protected* the trees and bushes and took revenge on those who violated or desecrated them. Such an idea was prevalent in Celtic belief to such an extent that even today in Ireland (and in some parts of Scotland), certain trees will not be touched for any purpose. A few years ago I spoke to an old man who lived near the small town of Kilrea in County Londonderry, who had worked in his youth as a surfaceman (a man who looked after and maintained rural roads). He told me that on one occasion, he had accidentally cut down part of a whitethorn tree (a growth sacred to certain sprites) that was growing in a roadside hedge. The next morning he had awoken to find that his spine had been twisted whilst he slept, and it remained so ever since. The doctors were at a loss to explain it, and eventually said it was some major spasm or seizure that he had suffered. However, he had no recollection of such an event. He never worked since, and when I spoke to him he was staying in a retirement home for the disabled. The event was, in his mind, unquestionably put down to the intervention of the "fairies" or the spirits of the tree into which he had accidentally cut.

It was, in many parts of Ireland, also considered extreme ill-luck to bring branches bearing the flowers of the whitethorn tree into a house for decoration. To do so was to bring the spirits of the tree— the "fairies"—into the building, or else they would follow the flowers in. Once in a house they would create mayhem both to the individuals there (sickness, financial misfortune) and to the building itself and the property therein (damage, rot). Far from being placid tree-dwelling fairies, they were believed to be wild and feral creatures who held a certain antipathy toward humans and toward human ways. Thankfully they largely ignored Humankind, except when their trees or foliage were damaged or desecrated. Then they would take extremely savage reprisals against the perpetrators and/or their families and loved ones. They were certainly to be respected and feared.

The idea of these tree creatures, in fact, forms the basis of the 1931 ghost story by the noted writer M.R. James (1862–1936)—*The Ash Tree*—in which venomous spider-like creatures inhabit a ghastly tree and subsequently invade a nearby house. Such creatures may also have their origins in Greek myth—James may have used a type of being known as the "meliae" as his model. These were ash-tree spirits that the writer Hesiod (eighth century BC) tells us sprang from a mixture of blood and semen when the god Chronus castrated Uranus in Greek myth. Although the name *meliae* is derived from the Greek word for "honey," they were not terribly friendly toward Mankind and may have taken delight in predicting individual deaths (making them the forerunners of the Fates for some folklorists). Hesiod, in his major epic poem *Works and Days* (written around 700 BC), goes on to state that a race of men sprang from the meliae—suggestive, perhaps, of an aboriginal race about which the classical writers knew.

Dark Fairies

The idea of an aboriginal race—perhaps possessing knowledge and skills which the "mainstream" races did not, and perhaps continuing down through the ages in some form or another—was to be found in many cultures. In most instances such groupings remained hidden away from the eyes of ordinary folk, forming secretive communities in relatively remote and inaccessible places. In fact, in societies such as Iceland, there is a long tradition of the *huldufolk*—"hidden people" or "hidden communities"—who coexist alongside standard settlements, but have very little to do with them. They are reputedly highly secretive in their ways and are the last remnants of an old race that existed in Iceland—and throughout the north—before the coming of the Irish monks, who initially settled in the country, or indeed before the Viking settlers.

Huldufolk and Alfar

According to a tradition promulgated by the monks, the origin of the huldufolk goes back into early biblical times. When they dwelt in the Garden of Eden, Adam and Eve had a number of children who were regularly inspected by God to make sure they were upstanding and pure. On one occasion, some of the children became very dirty, and, rather than let God see their uncleanness, Eve hid them away in a remote part of the Garden. God, who knew all things, realized that they were there and made a pronouncement—"What Man has hidden from God, God will hide from Man." The dirty children were ancestors of the huldufolk, so when Adam and Eve were driven out of the Garden, so were the huldufolk, who were then driven north to live away from others in the frozen lands of snow and ice. They seem to have settled in parts of Iceland and in the Faeroe Islands.

Originally, the huldufolk were described as being tall and reasonably handsome, with little differentiation between them and humans (they were the children of Adam and Eve, after all), but later descriptions depict them as much smaller, more misshapen, and with rather strange and pointed ears. They are now described by another name—*alfar* (the nearest equivalent being elves). However, there still appears to have been some sort of confusion in Icelandic folkloric terms between the huldufolk and alfar. A rule of thumb once common in

Dark Fairies

Iceland was that the alfar didn't drink coffee or eat bread, whereas the huldufolk did, because their food was closer to that of humans. Nevertheless debate still raged. The famous Icelandic folklorist Jon Arnason (1819–1888) asserted that the two terms were the same, but that alfar was a somewhat derogatory term. The German ethnographer Konrad von Maurer (1823–1902) suggested that the term *alfar* was a way to avoid calling the huldufolk by their proper name, because this implied that they were less than human. (A similar thought is employed in Ireland where it is unlucky to refer to "fairies" except on Tuesdays "when their heels are to you." The term that is used here is "the Good People.") An ethnographic survey conducted in 2006, however, found that few Icelanders made any distinction between the two.

The alfar constructed small stone houses in various remote parts of Iceland, which the local people called *alfhol* (roughly translated as "elf houses"). There they lived side by side with the Icelanders and seemed to enjoy an excellent relationship with them. Indeed, the alfar were invariably connected with fertility, were extremely lusty, and are said to have fathered a number of human children from Icelandic maidens. They were also associated with growing things, were incredibly good at horticulture, and observed many old traditions from the Pagan times, including festivals and dances. This would bring them into conflict with the Christian Church, which was spreading across Iceland and Faroes in the 11th and 12th centuries.

In the late 12th century there was a general opposition to dancing in Iceland, particularly at ancient festivals that occurred at certain times of the year. The movement was largely inspired by the Church, which saw such behavior as anti-religious. It was also the province of the huldufolk, whom the clerics viewed as secretive and sinister custodians of the old Pagan ways. In a number of tales from the period, either huldufolk or alfar joined with a number of local communities in order to oppose dancing bans (and the Church) and to restore old festivals. This, of course, made them implacable enemies of Christianity, and the Church decreed that they should be driven away from civilized Christianity and further into the wilds. Yet as late as the 15th century there are still stories of huldufolk aiding various villages in the preservation of their traditions, such as one tale in which the village overthrows a harsh sheriff who has placed a ban on dancing and festivals.

But relations between humans and huldufolk weren't always so cordial. Although there were a number of nights when the huldufolk congregated (especially during the winter—or "thick nights"—when the land was dark even during daytime and Icelanders believed that all manner of evils went about at this time), there were four human festivals that were particularly special to them. Three of these were around the same time in the Christian calendar—Christmas, Twelfth Night (January 6th), New Year's Eve, and Midsummer. At these times the huldufolk became particularly boisterous and often malignant in their ways and would often cause damage or injury to humans. They broke into houses, held impromptu parties, and often attacked the house-holders—some stories claim that they might even kill if provoked. In many cases it was claimed that many of these "parties" were of a sexual nature, with young girls being raped or otherwise sexually attacked.

Icelandic Lore

Around the 13th century, Iceland became slightly more accessible to the wider world. The literature of Iceland, which was composed of the Eddas (written largely by the monks at the early Icelandic monasteries) and poems became part of a wider spectrum, which was composed of bound books and other texts. Many of these contained the myths and legends of other cultures, and the beliefs of the Icelanders slowly began to change as a result. The huldufolk now diminished in size, became equated with dwarves and elves from other traditions, and took on some of their characteristics. They became slightly more sinister in the popular imagination and sometimes changed their habitations to deep caves and narrow ravines near the center of Iceland. Physically, they seemed to become more misshapen and demonic-looking and their attitude became more malignant and anti-human. Folklore concerning them began to evolve by portraying them in a less-than-flattering light, and special emphasis was placed (perhaps with the help of some clerics) on their misdeeds and evil nature. Names such as *jolasveinar* (Yule Lads) began to come up in some tales. These were creatures—sometimes said to be a branch of the huldufolk—

who came to houses when the long winter darkness was at its worst to steal away children from their cribs. Traditionally, they were said to be some of the 13 sons of the ogress and monster Gryla, who continually stirred a great pot deep in her cave in the mountains where she boiled up the flesh of captured children into a tasty stew. The idea of the ogress and her 13 sons is very old, and they are even mentioned in a 13th-century prose poem by the Icelandic historian and writer Snorri Sturluson (1178–1241). So widespread and terrifying was this belief that all mention of Gryla and her offspring was forbidden in Iceland and the Faeroes by the Church, punishable by imprisonment, under a general law in 1746. Nevertheless, stories and legends concerning them still abounded all across Iceland.

And there were other fairy horrors too, such as like the *gluggagaegir* or "Window Peeper," a terrible creature with large eyes that peered in at the windows of houses intent on stealing young children (or indeed the old and frail). It would remove them to its cave in the mountains where it would feed upon them, ripping them to shreds with long and deformed claws. Allied to this was the *askaluiker* or "Bowl Licker," which broke into houses and ate the food from the larders. It had a particular liking for herring (part of the Icelanders' staple diet) and could kill if it was interrupted. These night horrors, together with a number of others, were sometimes believed to be huldufolk, and stories concerning them show how much the perception of these "hidden people" was changing. No longer were they the allies of local communities, helping in keeping the traditional ways alive; rather, they were dark, Pagan entities intent on doing Mankind harm.

Trolls

Another variation of the "hidden people" was the trolls, who were considered to be the misshapen offspring of giants who had once ruled in the northern lands. The idea may have been a fusion of myths associating the huldufolk with perhaps another aboriginal race. It is possible that this may have been imported from another culture because the word *troll* seems to have its origins in the Germanic *trolldom* (meaning witchcraft) or *trylle* (a trickster or one who performs magic tricks), although the linkage is not firmly established. The word was applied to any uncanny being that lived away from men, usually in clefts and caves. They varied in size from diminutive beings to large creatures who were the direct offspring of the *jottnar*, or giants. They were usually vicious and brutish, although some of them could be extremely sly and devious.

Vitterfolk

There was some debate as to what trolls might actually be—whether they were Icelandic huldufolk or Swedish vitterfolk. The two might superficially appear as variants of one another (indeed some folklorist class them both as a form of *huldra*—a different being from humans), but there are subtle differences. For example, whereas the huldufolk were usually diminutive and elf-like, the vitterfolk were tall, good-looking, and almost indistinguishable from humans save in one respect—they had a tail. They often concealed their tail inside their clothing, so that it would not be detected when they passed for Humankind. Their basic nature, however, was that of the troll, and their powers were supernatural. For instance, they could sometimes change shape—usually taking the form of birds, animals, or inanimate objects such as fallen logs—or become invisible (when they would enter houses in order to do mischief).

Most trolls, however, were considered to be extremely primitive and often of limited intelligence, living in the wild and on what they could catch. In order to hunt, they could sometimes alter their size and become either giants or dwarves. Some of them lived isolated existences in caves and ravines, but other smaller variants lived in communities in underground burrow complexes. These might be accessed from underneath large rocks and boulders, or from narrow trails deep in the forests. It was into these underground warrens that captives were taken and sexually abused, used as slaves, or even used as food by the troll creatures. Those who were carried off were known widely as *bergtagna*, which means "taken to the mountain" but was more generally used for being "spirited away." This name even referred to those who had been either rescued or returned, because their experience among troll society had left them changed—either insane or "strange" in some way, and not really a part of their former communities. Women who were brought back pregnant were taken immediately to the local church for a blessing, and when the child was born it was taken away and placed under the dominion of clerics in remote monasteries and convents. People who had been among the trolls were considered "tainted" and were usually shunned. Trolls and humans did not mix, and the former were considered to be the very antithesis of all that was decent and human.

It is easy to see how such beliefs came into being; large parts of Iceland were (and still are) uninhabited, and contained traces of early volcanic activity. Such upheavals have created bizarre and twisted geographical landscapes, which, in the uncertain light of the northern skies, often created false impressions; the suggestion is that these shadows might be living things. Oddly shaped rocks, for instance, may have been mistaken for gnomes or trolls, and certain features in the landscape might have appeared to be strange dwellings that vanished when approached. Such occurrences might then be incorporated into supernatural story and legend. It is no coincidence that many trolls were considered to be the embodiment of the landscape just as the huldufolk were.

The Mounds

There were also the mounds, erected by former peoples, that throughout the centuries began to attract certain stories about them. They were, it was said, the abode of trolls and huldufolk who needed to be placated and worshipped. Local communities attempted to do so by leaving offerings and staging ceremonies at the mounds. So widespread was the practice that in 1276 the Norwegian King Manus Hakonssen or Hakonarson (Magnus VI, 1238–1280) was forced to issue a decree making such practice illegal and punishable by death. No one, he declared, was to "disturb or wake the mound dwellers," for fear they would take revenge on the kingdom—a jurisdiction that extended as far as the Faeroe Island and Shetland.

The basis of Magnus's edict was the theory that some of these "dwellers" may have been related in some way to the dead (there was a growing theory around this time that "fairies" and the dead were in some ways the same), and that the offerings were being left at the tombs of dead warriors. There were, scattered across the Scandinavian countryside, small stone "houses" in which the corpses of great chieftains or mighty warriors lay, and it was thought that these might be somehow supernaturally changed into "fairy-like" beings or into some form of huldur, which would take revenge on certain communities if disturbed. Many of the mounds also came from a more ancient time and may have been raised by vanished races, perhaps as funerary sites. Some communities viewed such places with awe and more than a little dread. These, they asserted, were places where old powers, long forgotten, still survived, and might be harmful to those who had anything to do with them. Thus, even vegetables that grew too near to these mounds were considered "tainted" with ancient fairy magic and were not to be eaten; nor was the fruit of any tree that grew nearby. Such food would have dangerous effects not only on the individual concerned but also on the whole community. They were probably, it was said, blighted by some long-vanished race, the remnants of which might still be around, and who were perhaps hostile toward those who had come to the land after them. These were still the huldufolk, the hidden people, now equated with the enemies of Mankind.

Hildaland

Hidden people were also associated in Norwegian folklore with Hildaland, an invisible continent that lay somewhere to the south. This legendary place was never seen, although pieces of it appeared from time to time as small islands, which later vanished again. These "pieces" could have possibly been great whales and sea creatures glimpsed in the poor light. Though according to some tales the majority appeared to seafarers roughly once every seven years. The people of Hildaland were skilled boatmen and went about in flat-bottomed crafts, which they sailed close to their own shores. They were often described as "wanderers" or "nomads" using the invisible country simply as a summer habitation and wintering elsewhere. From time to time, however, they raided along the coasts of nearby lands (usually at night) carrying away children and food back to Hildaland. In some tales, the invisible country was no paradise, but was described as a pitted, volcanic wasteland of caves and rough villages where the "fairies" lived.

By all accounts they appear to have been a pretty primitive and savage people very much in the style of troll society. Some stories describe them as small and covered in hair, although others say that they are tall and slender and with long tails. They were the last remnants of an ancient people who had once ruled the world, it was said. Other accounts of the mystical land, however, describe it as a pleasant place of lakes and streams where humans who visited it would forget their own land. But it was a realm that travelers should have avoided, and some versions of it would later merge into stories of "fairyland"—a wonderful place just beyond human vision from which the inhabitants came and went into the wider world, and from which few human wanderers ever returned, held there forever by its ancient inhabitants.

Grogochs

The idea of small, hairy, near-inhuman beings appears in other traditions besides the Nordic, although it is possible that there has been some Viking influence in the formation of such tales. On Ireland's North Antrim coast, for instance, there are references to the grogoch—a small pygmy, extremely primitive, completely naked, but wholly covered in a thick reddish hair. Descriptions of them are generally consistent—making them roughly the height of a two-year-old child with a wizened face like a monkey. Similar to the trolls, such beings dwell in caves or in structures known as "grogoch's houses" (similar to the *alfhol* of Iceland) and are reasonably sociable. They are supposed to be very affable, but believed to be not very bright and not very hygienic. Indeed, the celebrated Waterfoot storyteller Mary Stone often stated that it was a common expression in the Glens of Antrim to say that someone's untidy hair made them "look like an oul' Grogoch" or that a dirty house was like "a Grogoch's midden (refuse heap)." But they were considered to be extremely hard workers and would work for nothing (in fact, if one was offered a reward for work, it would simply vanish away), except a jug of buttermilk, which it downed with gusto. Many Antrim farmers were eager to use them as laborers at certain times of the year, such as harvest time when

they worked from dawn till dusk for no wages. Grogochs are said to be extremely helpful and friendly, and as such were often quite easily taken advantage of. Contrast them with the *loughremen* of South Armagh (who look similar), who are said to guard hidden ecclesiastic treasures and are said to be extremely ferocious, killing interlopers on their domain if need be in order to protect their wealth.

But were these creatures actually "fairies"? In both North Antrim and South Armagh it would appear so—in fact, both were given as a species of leprechaun. They were alleged to have at least some supernatural powers, such as the power of invisibility and the ability to move material objects without touching them; they were also believed to go without sleep and to sustain themselves without eating for long periods. To some this was evidence of their fairy origins. However, a rather fierce debate on the matter rages because some tales cited them as another species of man. And therein lay the heart of the problem with ancient perceptions of fairies. Not only were they another (and perhaps separate) race of creatures, but they were in fact a form of mirror image of ourselves. Perhaps, argued some, they had been created by God as a precursor to Mankind—a trial run or prototype, if you like. In fact, what if the fairies were actually our supernatural (or at least slightly more evolved) ancestors or distant "cousins"?

Adam Kadmon

In a number of ancient religious and philosophical traditions—Eastern, Arab, and Hebrew amongst them—it was asserted that the Divine Creator had created a prototype man before the creation of Humankind. Some of the texts of the mystical Jewish Kabbalah, for example, speak of Adam Kadmon, a kind of Universal being whom Yahweh (the Creator) made well before the creation of Man. This creation was in fact an emanation of Yahweh himself, which had taken material shape, and it was through this being that the Creator fashioned the first humans. The Upanishads also speak of a similar being—"a man of light"—that was an emanation of the Divine and which had Divine attributes. What became of these "first men" is unknown—perhaps they were taken back into the Divine being or became angels or some similar entity (in many cultures these creatures did not "know death"), but it is possible that the idea evolved so that they became beings in their own right and not simply manifestations of the Divine Being. Nevertheless, in their original state as emanations of the Infinite they had aided the Divine Being in the creation of the world, and to do this they had used wonderful powers (which in some variations they had been specially given by the Creator), which they retained. Thus, the original Adam Kadmon was reputedly as "human" as ourselves, albeit in a wider context.

Tuatha de Danann

The transformation of this ideal into that of a strange, mystical, and supernaturally powerful race is perhaps most evident in Ireland. Reference to the Tuatha de Danann, an early Irish race, is to be found in the *Lebor Gabala Erenn* (the *Book of the Taking of Ireland*, also known in English as *The Book of Invasions* or the *Book of Conquests*) a collection of extremely ancient texts compiled sometime around the 11th century by an unknown scholar. It seeks to set a timeline of the settlement of Ireland from prehistoric times until the arrival of Christianity, but in all actuality it comprises history, mythology, and folklore, recounting all these elements as if they were historical fact, detailing a number of races (who may or may not have actually existed) who colonized the land before recorded history.

One of these was the Tuatha de Danann, a race of quasi-supernatural beings whom many people have suggested were the forerunners of Irish fairies. They made up a fifth of the race that settled in the country, and their influence was said to have been profound. Their name is of course open to question—it is usually given as "the Children or People of the Goddess Danu," but this is not strictly true.

The term *Tuath* in ancient Irish certainly refers to a people or to the land held by them, but the term *de* or *dia* in Indo-European script can refer to a god or goddess. These were either a godly people or else the emanations of a god or goddess. And there is some dispute as to exactly who the Goddess Danu was. The Tuatha were said to come from the East in a golden cloud, driving out the established inhabitants of Ireland—the Fir Bolgs (Bagmen)—and calling on their Mother Danu for help. This would seem to suggest that Danu was an

Eastern goddess. Indeed, in Hinduism *Danu* is a name for the goddess Asura whose nature is given as that of the Primeval Waters from which all life proceeded. In other words, she would appear to be the First Mother and Divine Creator. But the name is very ambiguous and may also come from a Celtic word meaning "to flow," which once again suggests primordial waters. (This is the root of the name of the River Danube in Europe, which flows through an area that was once colonized by Celtic peoples.) There have also been suggestions that the word may mean "land" and that it is connected closely with nature and fertility. In all cases she is the source of birth and life. Her "children or people" could therefore be seen as emanations of this water or earth deity who have taken on human form. According to tradition, there was no real physical distinction between the Tuatha and human beings, with the possible exception that the Tuatha were perfect in every way and boasted a golden-tinged skin, denoting their Eastern origin. However, it was their knowledge and powers that set them apart from Humankind. As a race, they possessed a prodigious occult knowledge that covered such aspects as healing, warfare, agriculture, and metalworking. And they seemed to be strongly connected with the natural world, being skilled in the use of herbs and potions, with a phenomenal knowledge of plants and their uses. They were superior to other races in learning and craft.

It is unclear when exactly the Tuatha de Danann arrived in Ireland—the *Lebor Gabala* is not specific (although another later work, the 17th-century *Annals of the Four Masters,* suggests that they might have reigned in Ireland between 1897 BC and 1700 BC)—but it is traditionally said that they came in or around May 1st, which, of course, corresponds to the ancient Celtic festival of Beltane. They fought two great battles—the First and Second Battles of Magh Tuiredh (Moytura), one in County Galway and one in County Sligo. One was against the Fir Bolg and the other against a race known as the Fomorians, who are often equated with the giants or Titans of classical myth. Both they won easily by virtue of their magical arts and cunning warcraft—although not without some significant casualties. According to the texts, they were less successful against a subsequent wave of invaders known as Milesians, who came from the areas of Portugal and Galicia (the Iberian Peninsula). They were the last race to inhabit Ireland, according to the *Lebor*. Again, the date of their arrival in the country is unknown, but it was said to predate 1,000 BC The war between the two factions more or less resulted in a stalemate, and an agreement was finally reached: The Milesians would inhabit a greater part of the country and the Tuatha the more remote and underground areas. They were led away to their new realm by one of their leaders, the Dagda (often equated with an old prehistoric Irish god), into the caves, mounds, and tumuli that dotted the country. As Milesian society expanded, the Tuatha became more and more reclusive (although they had taught certain of the invaders some of their arts), and gradually all contact between the two races more or less stopped. In later legend, the Tuatha—the godly people—became equated with the fairies, even though they were supposed to be another, more mystical form of human. From time to time, however, the Tuatha married into the Milesians (who were now identified as misplaced Spanish Celts) and bore offspring, for there was no actual physiological difference between the two races.

And yet, according to Irish folklore, the Tuatha still harbored an enmity toward those who had displaced them. In their mounds and forts, they often conspired and fulminated against those who had taken over the greater portion of the country that they had once ruled. They plotted ways to do them harm and, as they retained their former supernatural powers and specialized knowledge, they were sometimes able to achieve this. They became, in effect, evil fairies and creatures with whom all right-thinking and Godly people should have no contact. They were, it was asserted, the remnants of an old and Pagan society that had long passed away—the emanations, in human form, of a goddess who had been all but forgotten.

So, what were perhaps the last remembrances of another aboriginal species—Neanderthals or something else—that had perhaps formed the basis for a belief in huldufolk, now became tinged with visions of a quasi-divine race (perhaps the descendants of a prototype man, such as Adam Kadmon), creating a reclusive supernatural community that often shunned Mankind and which might regard and treat them as enemies. Stories regarding former or "elder races" circulate in legends and are to be found in religion, philosophy, and literature. The Bible, for instance, makes reference to "the Sons of God," who found the daughters of Men fair and who mated with them (Genesis 6: 1–4), although it is not specific as to what these beings were. Madame Blavatsky made reference to a number of "root races" that had existed on Earth long before humans—in places like Atlantis, Lemuria, and Mu—while the American writer H.P. Lovecraft created an entire genre out of the notion of ancient races still slumbering beneath the New England landscape. Might these have been some fragment of a memory of ancient species akin to the Tuatha de Danann that somehow lingered on somewhere in the back of the human mind?

Because these beings might be another form of Humankind, Irish fairy society (and often that of England, Scotland, and Wales) in many ways reflected that which our forebears knew and with which they could identify. Similar to the huldufolk they often dwelt in recognizable houses in North Antrim and on Rathlin Island, where there are identifiable structures made of stone that are known as "Grogoch's houses." Their social structure was organized in the same way as that of Humankind, with a king and a queen at its head; they argued and fought amongst themselves, and they sometimes farmed and kept livestock. They also enjoyed parties and balls that were held within "fairy hills" and "fairy forts." In many respects the social network of these fairies mirrored that of their Irish counterparts. Despite all this similarity, there was also a darker element amongst fairy kind.

Macara Shee

In his essays on folklore, the Irish poet and writer W.B. Yeats often spoke of the *Macara Shee* (the trooping fairies or the Fairy Cavalcade). This was a parade of fairies that supposedly wandered the Irish roads at certain times of the year (usually under cover of darkness) as the king and queen of a local region surveyed their territory. It was usually a frivolous procession, full of merriment and humor but there were also difficulties when it met with local people who happened to be out and about. It depended on the humor of the fairies as to what happened then—they could perhaps take the person whom they met with them, into the fairy hills and mounds where they would never be seen again, or, if they were in a good humor they might dispense largesse by handing out money or jewels. Mainly, however, the disposition of the fairies to those whom they met on the nightbound roads was of the former kind.

According to both Yeats and the folktale collector Lady Gregory, there was one particular sort of fairy who traveled with the Cavalcade that was particularly dangerous. This was the *Amadan-na-Briona* or Fool of the Forth. He was said to be a trickster or a jester and was evilly disposed toward humans.

"I have heard one Hearne, a witch-doctor who is on the border of Clare and Galway," wrote Yeats in *The Celtic Twilight* (1893), "say that in 'every household of faery there is a Queen and a Fool and that if you are touched by either, you never recover though you may from the touch of any other in faery.' He said of the Fool that he was 'maybe the wisest of all' and spoke of him 'dressed like the mummers that used to be going about the country.' Since then a friend has gathered a few stories of him and I have heard that he is known in the Highlands. I remember seeing a long, lank, ragged man sitting by the hearth in the cottage of an old miller not far from where I am now writing and being told that he was a Fool." He went on to say that this individual "became" a fairy when he slept—he was, in fact, "possessed" by the fairy spirit—and ventured forth along the roads (whether in actuality or in dreams) to attack his neighbors. The Fool carried with him a wand or rod with which he delivered his "touch," and took away the power and reason of those whom he tapped with it. The word for such an action was a "stroke"—a taking away of the strength and power from the individual—and this has given us the medical term that we still use today.

A stroke occurs when the blood supply to the brain is disturbed or interrupted and functioning brain cells begin to die, causing power loss and even death in a number of instances. This was the terrible power that the Fool's wand could deliver, and in a society that had no medical explanation for such a condition, the intervention of the hostile fairy served as an explanation for these difficulties. The fairy was never seen, but delivered his touch invisibly. Yet the folklore around the Fool of the Forth was widespread, even into the 20th century.

In her seminal book *Visions and Beliefs in the West of Ireland* (1920), Lady Augusta Gregory writes of how she interviewed a Sligo oyster woman about the Fool on her way back from a local seashore:

> There was a boy, one Rivers, got the touch last June from the Amadan-na-Briona, the Fool of the Forth, and for that touch there is no cure. It came to the house in the night-time and knocked at the door and he did not rise to let it in. And it knocked the second time and even then if he had answered it, he might have escaped. But when it knocked the third time, he fell back on the bed and one side of him as if dead and his jaw fell on his pillow. He knew it was the Amadan-na-Briona did it but he did not see him—he only felt him. And he used to be running in every place after that and trying to drown himself and he was in great dread that his father would say he was mad and bring him away to Ballinasloe. He used to be asking could his father do that to him. He was brought to Ballinasloe after and he died there and his body was brought back and buried at Drumacoo.

In my youth I remember knowing of a man who lived a little distance away from us who was widely regarded as being "possessed" by the Fool of the Forth, and who, when in that state, could deliver the "touch," which would paralyze. He was a strange, solitary man who lived alone in a small house in the middle of a bog and he was said to be "odd" in his ways. According to local tradition, he was married at one time with a family some distance away. Being very fond of a "bottle or two" (strong drink) he had become intoxicated one night at a party and on the way home had paused to sleep it off on the edge of a fairy fort near the roadside. While lying there inebriated, the Amadan had come upon him and had "possessed" him, and he had never been the same again. He left his wife and family and went off to live in the cottage, which had belonged to his brother. It was said that it was for their own good, for his touch when the fairy "possession" was upon him was lethal. Then he was not counted as being human but was simply "more than human," connected to another species of Man or a part of a mystical race such as the Tuatha de Danann. He was now the Fool of the Forth. But for many of our neighbors he was also a madman, for the fairy "possession" had taken away his wits and had made him "strange" or "not normal," and children like myself were terrified of him. My grandmother often used this man as a warning of what strong drink would do to a person vis-à-vis a relationship with the fairies, for it was well known that the overconsumption of liquor drew creatures such as the Fool of the Forth to an individual. This "interchangeability" showed the close relationship that existed between fairies and humans and hinted that, at a very basic level, they might be connected in some way.

Fear Gorta

In some instances, too, human history and fairy belief mingled in the persona of the fairy. This could be seen in the Fear Gorta (the Man of Hunger), a creature that, akin to the Fool of the Forth, was best to avoid. The belief in the Fear Gorta seems to have grown up in Ireland in the years following the Great Potato Famine (1845–1852), although the idea of the being itself may be much older. And like the Fool of the Forth, the Fear Gorta tramped the Irish roads passing from house to house. Emaciated, he seemed more like a skeleton than a fairy, and seemed to be the very epitome of the Famine hunger. He carried two things with him: a long staff on which he leaned and a small tin alms cup with which he would beg from the houses that he passed by. Within the cup he had a single coin, which he would rattle in order to signal his presence. Late in the evening, as families gathered around their fires, the faint chink of the tin cup at the back door was the sign that the fairy desired a gift or alms. The woman of the house would maybe rise and go to the back door with a crust of bread or a scrap of meat and leave it on the back doorstep for the being who waited there invisibly. If this was done then the family enjoyed prosperity and good health for the coming season; if it was not, then misfortune would surely follow. Similarly, if one were to meet with the Fear Gorta upon the road in the guise of an emaciated beggar, it was bad luck to refuse the tin cup that the fairy thrust out and not to give it some form of offering. If this was not done, great misfortune and even death would inevitably follow.

Although the image of this particular fairy unquestionably lies in the Famine Era in Ireland, it may actually have much older origins. The offering that is given to it may contain echoes of the offerings given to older gods or to the quasi-divine beings, such as the Tuatha de Danann, by our ancestors in former times. Even as late as the latter years of the 19th century (and indeed perhaps the late 20th century) people still left gifts of flowers and food at ancient tumuli and mounds in order to honor or placate the people who were believed to dwell within them. This may have come from a time when quasi-supernatural beings such as the Tuatha de Danann were regarded as something akin to deities, or it may suggest that in the popular mind relations between the two races were not considered to be all that friendly, and the supernatural species might readily turn on the other if not appeased in some way. The notion of dark "fairies" living in these places, ready to do their distant relations harm, might have been extremely widespread. This may also have been prevalent in the image of the Fear Gorta who demanded (and received) some form of offering from people whom he met or whose houses he passed. The sole purpose of such an offering was to ward away supernatural evil.

Banshees

Besides being connected with early proto-races, which had existed long before Mankind, fairies also had a strong connection with the human dead. One of the most famous fairies associated with this aspect of fairy lore in both Irish and Scottish folklore is the banshee (*bean sidhe)* or "woman of the fairy," whose appearance often signaled the death of members of great clans or families within the Gaelic world. In Scotland, she often appeared as an old woman washing clothes at the side of a river. The Washer at the Ford—an embodiment perhaps of the Celtic death goddess Coltha, who has given her name to the River Clyde. In Ireland she sometimes is described as a screaming hag whose wailing often foretold the demise of a specific family member. She too was associated with tumuli and mounds, as she was often thought to be an emissary of the "hidden people," taking a perverse delight in the demise of humans.

Dark Fairies

In her book *Gods and Fighting Men* (1910), Lady Gregory makes reference to a fairy woman named Aiobhaill (the Lovely One) who was a banshee to the Royal House of Munster and to its ruling O'Brien clan. She is said to have dwelt on the Rock of Craig Laith (Craiglea) in County Clare, close to the ancestral seat of the O'Brien family, from which she uttered prophesies. These prophecies helped the kings of the area to rule. She foretold a number of battles in Ireland during the 10th and 11th centuries, including the great Battle of Clontarf near Dublin between the Irish king Brian Boruma (Brian Boru) and the Vikings on Good Friday, 1014. According to legend, she fell in love with Dublaig ua Artigan (Dunlang O'Hartigan), a Dalcassian captain from County Clare who served in Brian's army, and, knowing that he and his sons would be killed during the battle, she offered him many years of life and greatness if he would refuse to take part in the fighting for a single day. Loyal to his king, O'Hartigan refused and was killed on the battlefield the following evening. Heartbroken, Aiobhaill returned to Craiglea where her cry can still be heard today. Interestingly, however, some variants of the tale state that one of O'Hartigan's sons who was killed with him on the battlefield had been fathered from the banshee and therefore was Aiobhaill's own offspring. This would seem to suggest that the Banshee was an ordinary woman—capable of mating with a mortal man.

It is also said that Aiobhaill foretold the death of Brian Boru, and because of this the king (who was more than 70 years old at the time) took no part in the battle. He was, however, killed in the doorway of his tent by an axe thrown by Brodr, a Viking king from the Isle of Man, as he waited for news of the conflict. Again it was said that Aiobhaill had been the king's lover (fairy women were often considered incredibly promiscuous) and this dealt her a double blow, causing her to withdraw from the recognizably mortal world.

Places such as ancient Ireland and ancient Scotland were made up of a number of petty kingdoms, which were frequently at war, and, consequently, these lands were very violent. Local kings, often little more than warlords, frequently tried to extend their dominions by invading those of their neighbors. Now it was advantageous to know whether such conquests would be victorious or indeed whether the local ruler would live to fight another day. To do this, he needed to know the future, and possibly for this purpose he consulted with a woman with special prognosticary powers—a banshee—who could advise him. It is also possible that, because of her alleged powers, such a female was counted as one of the spirit or fairy race—the Tuatha de Danann. In fact, such women may have held special status within the noble households of Ireland. This is probably the root of the belief that the banshee cries only for those who die within the great houses. An ancient Irish text, the *Coir Anmann* (perhaps written around the 12th or 13th centuries) makes a brief reference to the Banshee of the Royal House of Munster (could this have been Aiobhaill?) who was sought after by the Dalcassian kings and who prophesied for them on many things.

Nor was the ability to "see death" ascribed solely to the ancient women of history. In his book *Travels in Ireland*, German tourist Johann Kohl describes how he was taken to see an 80-year-old woman living in a cabin close to where he was staying. This woman, whom he names as Cosideen, had the ability to see death, leaning on two sticks at the foot of an adjoining meadow and peering through the hedges when any of her family were about to die. This ancient woman was regarded as something of a banshee by her local community and was considered to be extremely important by her neighbors. Similarly, in the West of Scotland and in the Western Isles there are still a number of people who claim to be able to see approaching death or disaster through the "second sight" or the "taish," as they sometimes refer to it.

So the original banshee may have been something of a seeress attached to some of the great Irish houses, and may have been an actual living person; so how did she become the wailing phantom of popular literature? How did she become bitter and hostile toward those whose death she foretold, as she appears in some tales? Perhaps it was through her foretelling of and close association with death itself. In earlier times the Church, in order to obtain money from its congregations, warned that the dead might be hostile toward the living. It was the custom among the clergy to say Masses for the dead—for the continuing repose of their souls—on the anniversary of their death in return for a fee (this practice is still carried on in Ireland and other places). If the relatives or descendants were to forget to pay the priest and the Masses were left unsaid, then the spirit of the dead individual might return in order to take vengeance against them. The dead envied the living, so they might even have done physical harm or at the very least bring them misfortune. And so the dead became imbued with a kind of "evil," as did those entities that were associated with them—such as the banshee.

Keening

Her cry was closely associated with the Irish form of "keening," or professional mourning at a funeral or wake. To emphasize the status of the deceased within the community some families in both Ireland and Scotland actually employed women to follow the coffin and to shriek and cry uncontrollably as if in terrible grief. This practice stretched back into Pagan Celtic times when professional mourners followed the corpse of some powerful chief or great warrior to his final resting place, beating their breasts and screaming. Many clergy found such demonstrations "false and showy," as a relic of Pagan times, and treated them with contempt. Indeed, in 1645, the Church of Scotland placed a ban on wakes in which professional keening was a part, declaring it to be "vain and presumptuous," and forbidding its clergy to officiate at all services at which such keeners were in evidence.

The Irish Church was not far behind, and in 1669 the Primate of Armagh placed a similar ban on all such Irish funerals and wakes—especially within the Armagh area in which it seemed to have been exceedingly popular. In 1670, the Synod of Armagh reinforced the Bishop's ruling that all keening at funerals was "unchristian." (They were reiterating an edict from the Synod of Tuam in 1631, which had explicitly forbidden "exaggerated crying" at funerals.) Of course, people still continued with this custom, but now it was denounced by the Church as a thing of evil and was associated with dark Paganism, and it would become associated with the banshee. Her cry now became a gloating, screeching call of triumph, rather than the sweet and harmonious singing it had previously been. It seemed now as if she was actually rejoicing in a human death, and the sound was a thing to be feared. Far from being the mystical seeress, warning of future events, she had become a creature that lay some way between a ghost and a fairy. She had drifted into the realm of dark and malignant beings.

Leprechauns

There were other types of Irish fairies who fell into this category and who might have been associated with former vanished races, some of them quite surprising. Among those beings, whom W.B. Yeats classed as "solitary fairies," was the leprechaun. Traditionally, he (for these fairies always appear to be male) is counted as a jolly little fellow full of mischief, but kindly at heart. Far from the general impression, often endorsed by the Irish Tourist Board, however, the leprechaun may be a shy and surly creature, who may do harm to mortal people if he can.

Despite its now more widespread appeal—it is now often used to describe any type of Irish fairy—the term *leprechaun* was not really used until the late 17th or 18th centuries. Even then, the word had several localized variations. In East Leinster, for example, the term was *liomreachan*, while in South Leinster it was *luracan*; in Ulster it was *luchraman,* in Connacht *lurican*. And even within the Provinces themselves, the name often varied. For instance, in parts of Munster, the fairy was called a *luchargan, lurgadan*, or *clurican*, whereas in some districts the term *luchorpan* prevailed. The origin of the name "leprechaun" is complex. It has been argued that it derives from *leith bhrogan* (half-shoe maker—the maker of half a pair of shoes), thus making the leprechaun a cobbler by profession and generating a corpus of related folklore around him. However, it is more likely that the term comes from the ancient Irish *luchorpan* (little man) or *luacharman* (pygmy), simply denoting a creature of very small stature. In a number of texts dating from around the eighth century, the term is used to describe a number of diminutive races living (or who were thought to be living) in Ireland. This explanation seems to be borne out by another name given to the leprechaun—pecht (also meaning a small, painted man in Scotland)—and gives credence to the idea that they are perhaps from a different species of man.

In the story of Fearghus MacLeide, for instance (possibly written around the 11th century, but recounted in Raphael Holinshed's *Chronicles* of

1577 and reprinted in Joseph Dunn's *The Glories of Ireland* in 1914), reference is made to such a community living in the West of Ireland, who exhibit supernatural powers. Fearghus captures three of them (including their king), and in return for letting them go he receives power, which transforms him into a miraculous swimmer. Other ancient texts from the same period stated that these small men had wonderful silver shoes, which enabled them to walk across the surface of water—that may have been how the idea of the leprechaun being a cobbler arose.

In the majority of books and films, the leprechaun is portrayed as a jolly little fellow, full of merriment and always ready for a laugh. In most folklore, he is somewhat different from that. He is a sober, solitary creature, often jealous and secretive about himself and his origins to the point of defensive violence. Nor is he portrayed in wider Irish folklore solely as a shoemaker (indeed that seems to be the least of his professions)—he is a distiller, a metalworker or smith, and, most importantly, a banker. Because of their long lifespan, leprechauns know where most of the ancient treasures of Ireland are hidden—gold that was hidden from Viking raids, fortunes that were buried during the Cromwellian period, and church rents that were put away during the penal times. These he guarded with an intense ferocity, either diverting, or in some instances, physically harming those who ventured too close. As has been already mentioned, the *loughremen* of South Armagh, thought to be a species of leprechaun, who were said to guard the hidden treasures of the old Kings of Ulster at Navan Fort, were believed to actually *kill* anyone who came looking for this wealth. According to W.B. Yeats, as the Macara Shee—the Fairy Cavalcade—traveled the roads of a night, they sometimes dispensed largesse to some of those mortals whom they met, usually in the form of gold or precious stones. In order to do this, they first had to approach the leprechaun in order to release part of the vast fortunes—the location of which he readily knew. He, with a heart as hard as any banker and with an innate dislike for humans (and other fairies as well) often gave only grudgingly and in the smallest amounts. This may be the origin of the belief that every leprechaun possesses a "crock of gold," which he has hidden away somewhere, and which others (particularly humans) are trying to find.

The idea of the leprechaun in all his variants may also hint, once again, at the idea of another race of people living alongside humans, perhaps in some former time. They seem to be embodiments of some shy, furtive, and reclusive people whom our ancestors all but forgot, but nevertheless incorporated into their folklore. And indeed there are stories of similar small peoples from parts of the world other than Ireland or Scotland. Among the Cherokees in Virginia and North Carolina, for instance, legends of the *nunnehi* (little people) are prevalent. These are mysterious little folk who live in the deep forests (often in ancient mounds), and who are, at best, rather mischievous, and at worst, downright evil. They make their presence known by shrill, fluting cries among the undergrowth, which are often feared by Cherokee and other Native American hunters.

German folklore also speaks of *kobolds,* or little (sometimes ugly) men who lived in small houses in the woods or in deep caves in the mountains, and also of the *heinzelmannen* tiny men who are specifically associated with the city of Cologne, who are so small that they can live in the foundations of old buildings. All of these are associated with groups of diminutive folk who may have come from an earlier time and have survived into our own. All of them are shy and elusive, and may do humans some form of harm if allowed.

Dwellings

Naturally, apart from one or two groupings, these diminutive forms of men tried to live as far away from Humankind as they could. They were associated with remote places: in Ireland old hill forts and raths that had been left over by previous peoples; in North Carolina the remote peaks and "balds" of the Smokies, which were the grounds of the *nunnehi*: old, abandoned graveyards and tombs (which inevitably associated them with the dead). They were known as "the people of the mounds," and certain areas of the rural countryside were considered to be specific to them. In fact, there were some areas where it was deemed inadvisable for humans to go.

Some of these places were located in such areas as the Western Isles of Scotland, such as on the tiny isles of Oronsay and Colonsay,

where, according to some sources, there were groups of blood-drinking fairies, somewhat akin to vampires. This was an area to which they had been consigned by the early Scottish saints and they could not leave it. But if anyone were to step into their territory (usually on remote parts of the islands) they did so at their own risk. Such places also existed in Ireland. Speaking at a conference in Trinity College Dublin in 1961, the Archivist of the Irish Folklore Commission, Sean O'Suilleabhain, mentioned a massive fortress that guarded a lonely trail in the Magillycuddy Reeks Mountains in Kerry. This place was known locally as Dun dreach-fhoula (the Castle of the Blood Visage) and was the habitation of a clan of vampiric fairies who preyed on travelers who passed by their walls. O'Suilleabhain was a Kerry man and had heard legends of the place when a child found bodies apparently drained of their blood beside lonely mountain trails. He also claimed that he knew exactly where the fortress was located and would reveal where it was at a subsequent lecture, but he never did. All attempts to find the location of the site have proved fruitless, and it does not appear on any land documentation concerning the Barony of Kilkerron, in which most of the Magillycuddy Reeks Mountains lie. And yet some tales concerning it persist. So does the fortress of blood-drinking fairies actually exist along some lonely mountain trail, or does it simply lie in the imaginations of local folklorists and storytellers? And are the mounds and hills in Ireland, the Western Isles, and beyond simply gateways into a dark realm where such creatures may still dwell—the last remnants of a lost race, continually plotting against Mankind? Are the People of the Mounds still watching and waiting? And, although this is a chilling prospect, do other dark fairies also lurk elsewhere?

Chapter 2

The Host of the Air

very ancient tale from Pembrokeshire, Wales, runs as follows.

There was an old woman living in a small cottage close to the foot of the Frenni fawr, which is, as you know, a fairy-haunted mountain where no human should really set foot. However, the old dame was never bothered by her fairy neighbors until one night. On that occasion she was coming around the corner of her home carrying a bundle of sticks for the fire. It was late in the evening, but it was very calm and still. Suddenly, however, a great wind seemed to gust in, passing over the old woman's head as she struggled against it; as it swirled about her, the wind seemed to contain a million voices, all speaking, singing, or shouting in different pitches and tones. And in the middle of all this din, she heard a child crying somewhere far away. It cried so piteously that the old woman's heart was touched.

"Oh the Lord God save the poor child on such a windy night!" she cried aloud. At the mention of the Holy Name, the wind suddenly ceased and the child dropped like a stone from the heavens into her arms. Then she knew what had happened. The "wind" had been the Tylwyth Teg (the fairy people of Wales), who had stolen a human child from its crib and were transporting it to the top of the mountain above which was their abode. As they passed over her house, the utterance of God's name had caused them to lose their grip on the baby, allowing it to fall into the old woman's arms. The child was a girl, and, being so young, she had no recollection of who her natural parents were or where she had come from. Because she had been carried away by the fairies, she might have traveled for many miles—maybe even from beyond the borders of Wales. There was no way of knowing where she had come from, and so the old woman raised her as if she were her own daughter. However, even when she was a grown woman, she still looked up toward the summit of Frenni fawr with a wary stare, for she knew that up there, the fairies continued to dance and wheel, and that because she had been touched by them as a child, they might still do her harm.

Although the tale is set in Wales, similar stories exist in many other places, such as Ireland, Scotland, Cornwall, and even in North Carolina and the Middle East. At the core of such stories is an explanation for the unpredictability of nature and perhaps unusual familial circumstances as well. For example, as a small boy I was both frightened and fascinated by a bizarre, weak-minded girl who lived not far from our house along with two old bachelor brothers. Her story matched the previous story—she had fallen as a baby from a "fairy wind," which had passed over the house and into a nearby earthen fort when one of the brothers had mentioned the Holy Name. Again, not knowing where she had come from the brothers raised her as their own, and because she had been "gathered up" by the fairies, her mental faculties had been compromised, and she was regarded as being "not right." She was slow and backward in her ways, never attended school, and walked about the roads talking to herself and making strange noises. Her condition was considered to be a sure sign of fairy intervention— "the touch of the fairy." The story concerning her, as I learned much later, covered up some difficult and illegal family circumstances.

When I was old enough to understand I was told that there was once a sister living with the two brothers—she was now in a mental home somewhere—and the girl was hers. The father had been one of her brothers. Living away in such a remote area—their cottage lay at the end of a long lane that led through a bog—and seeing very few other people, relationships had become very heated and intense. Incest had reared its head, and this at the time could not have been talked about— it was a ghastly and shameful sin in our community, after all, and the brothers were fairly respectable men. Therefore, the story about the fairies and the "fairy wind" served as a ready explanation for the girl's existence. It also drew its authority from local tradition and folklore. On the edge of the bog, close to the cottage, stood the earthen walls of a fairy fort (probably some ancient Celtic fort from a previous time) and it was said that the fairies came and went from it invisibly in a swarm at all times of the day and night. They were like flocks of birds rising from and landing in the center of the earthworks. According to the brothers, their comings and goings were "a torment," and who knew what they might be carrying? The old men had found bags of lime, dead animals, cooking implements, and other assorted paraphernalia (even an old chest of drawers at one time), which had been stolen and later dropped along the edges of the bog by the flying host. However, they were much too afraid to go up to the old fort and do anything about this. They simply tolerated their fairy neighbors.

The girl continued to live with the brothers for some years, and in that time she wandered in the bog, calling strangely in what the brothers said was "the fairy tongue." She was only removed when one of the old men killed himself and the other was blinded by drinking "bad poteen" (illegal spirits), and the girl, left behind, was taken into care. However, the story that she'd been taken by the fairies and deposited with the two old men was still persistent in the countryside for many years afterward. The earthen fort from which they supposedly arose each night was still avoided by local people.

Flying Creatures

The idea of swarming fairies through the skies may well have its origins in the notion of elemental air spirits. In classical Greek and Roman thought, air, which philosophers such as Plato called *aether*, was one of the most universal and basic elements in the world. Indeed, some queried whether it was actually a constituent of the Divine Intelligence in one of its purest forms. It was the breath of the Infinite, which sustained life—could it be that it also boasted intelligence? And indeed, could such intelligence live in the aether and take on some form of quasi-physical shape? It is no coincidence that many of the earliest representations of spirits and supernatural forces—whether good or bad—are shown with wings and as flying creatures.

Nowadays, we tend to think of winged humanoids—maybe corresponding to the idea of fairies—in a somewhat angelic context. This may be where the idea of small, winged fairies that are kindly, generous beings originates, but angels, in the Semitic tradition at least, were indifferent beings, neither particularly kindly nor especially wicked.

Angels

In Hebrew folklore these beings are given as *malakh* (the word *angel* comes from a Greek rendering of *angelos*), and are used in ancient texts to describe beings with either supernatural or superhuman powers. They were said to be the messengers of Yahweh, and traveled between the Divine Realm and the world of men, carrying pronouncements and instructions. In some cases they also carried a flaming sword—the symbol of Yahweh's authority—to take his vengeance on a disobedient and wayward world or upon certain individuals within it. Although they are usually not described in any great physical detail; it was usually taken for granted that they had human form and that they could fly. "Each one," says Isaiah (6:2), recording a vision, "had six wings. With two he covered his face, with two he covered his feet and with two he flew." However, the term *angel* covers not only a humanoid messenger, but other flying creatures as well. The "angels" that Isaiah was describing may well have been creatures known as *seraphim*, which were not strictly messengers, per se. They were part of God's retinue and their main function was destruction. Indeed, they were creatures of fire—their name coming from the Hebrew word *seraph* meaning "to burn"—and were the equivalent of stormtroopers or shock battalions. They were extremely vicious and accountable to God alone, often bringing pestilence and torment on Mankind. Isaiah was not altogether sure if they were angels, and therefore didn't really count them as such. Nor did he identify the cherubim in an angelic fashion. These are usually shown as small babies with soft downy wings who appear to be the embodiment of innocence. This, of course, is a Victorian Anglicized version. The cherubim of Hebrew mythology were Sphinx-like creatures with human heads and the bodies of lions, together with powerful wings like those of eagles. The guardians at the gate of Assyrian Nineveh were probably the nearest representation of the cherubim that earthly artists could come up with. The prophet Ezekiel gives a vision of the chariot-throne of Yahweh (God) and of the imagery that surrounded it, including that of the cherubim:

"They had the likeness of a man. Each one had four faces, and each one had four wings, and their feet were straight feet, and the sole of their feet was like the sole of a calf's foot and they sparkled like the colour of burnished brass" (Ezekiel 1:5). Once again, he does not identify them as "angels," for there were other complex creatures clustering around God's throne.

Similar to brigades of soldiers, the seraphim and the cherubim traveled through the air in groups, descending like fighter planes on humans below and spewing fire and molten lava on those deserving of Yahweh's wrath. Clouds of them might descend on a city—legend says that they might have done so in the days before the Flood—leveling the buildings and frying the inhabitants. These creatures simply were not the benevolent beings that we usually ascribe to the throng around the Celestial Throne.

Even those angels who resembled humans were sometimes not particularly well-disposed toward men. The Bible tells us that after deceiving his blind father Isaac, Jacob (who had tricked his brother Esau out of his birthright) was returning with his family from the land of Canaan. He was told that Esau was coming to meet him with a great army and he sent tributes and gifts ahead to try to placate his brother. At a ford of the Jabbok River, which rose in the ancient land of Rabboth-ammon, he met and wrestled all night with a "man" whom the Scriptures describe as an "angel." In the contest, Jacob appeared to be winning until the "angel" touched "the socket of his hip," and it was suddenly dislocated, thus defeating him. Even so, Jacob was not slain by the stranger and he would later call the river crossing Penuel or Peniy'el, meaning "the face of the Lord," because he said that he had "looked on the face of the Lord and had lived."

This has led some biblical scholars to suggest that angels were emanations of the Supreme Being, perhaps very much in the style of Adam Kadmon to whom we referred earlier. The battle at Jabbok was, of course, not Jacob's first encounter with so-called "angels." Prior to the struggle he had beheld a vision "while he slept," which showed a ladder climbing into the air where a number of beings went up and down, as if to Heaven. "Jacob's ladder" would later take on mystical connotations in rabbinical lore, and served to suggest connections between the ethereal beings of the upper airs and the world of men.

Air spirits, it was suggested, were everywhere, moving invisibly on their wings above the world. And they could sometimes influence the world below through their powers; for example, they could sometimes inspire men to do great deeds, compose great poems, or do great evil.

Demons

It was not a great leap from the notion of indifferent angels to that of demons. The word derives from the ancient Greek *daimon* meaning "a supernatural being" (although not necessarily evil). For some of the playwrights or musicians of ancient Greece this could be the muse that led their work; for an artist or engineer daimons might manifest themselves in a moment of brilliance, for a general or military leader they might inspire a particular tactic and campaign. These daimons lived in the air all around and their influence could be profound. It was only with the rise of organized religion that their attentions came to be questioned, and for some they became suspect. They "possessed" people and robbed them of their wits and rational thought, which was not good; they also provoked them to do things that were sometimes against the perceived common good. They caused individuals to act against received teaching, which was also contrary to the laws of gods and men. Thus, they became things of evil whose sole purpose was to overthrow the natural order and to lead men and women astray. And like angels and the spirits of the air, they were everywhere.

Djinn

The Semitic notion of air spirits—malignant and otherwise—who manifest themselves to mortals from time to time is to be found in Arab folklore too. Here they were the *djinn,* the followers of Iblis who had been created by God out of the "smokeless fire." Although Iblis has often been equated with the Semitic Shaitan (Satan), the djinni were not necessarily wholly evil beings, but they were supernatural entities that were often inimical or indifferent toward humans. They also took on many guises, sometimes as birds or dogs, but more often they appeared as clouds of dust—miniature dust storms that seemed to be stirred up by the wind but often had a malignant intelligence about them. They usually inhabited remote valleys or desolate areas of the desert and were best to be avoided. Those who communicated with them were few and far between, and were often known as *kahins* or seers. These wild-looking men usually sat in the corner of the marketplace making unintelligible utterances, which were said to convey the thinking of the spirit-kind. Such men were often deemed to be mad, probably through their contact with the spirit kind. Others who approached them were often borne away by them—maybe they were even torn apart by what seemed to be fierce winds; the djinn were often behind the mighty dust storms that swept in from the deserts. There was no real explanation for the origin of the djinn—some legends said that they were something akin to fallen angels; some said that they were demons; others said that they were forces left over from the creation of the universe or that they were nature spirits that had existed from earliest times. It is said that they were created out of "the purest light" and not from clay (as we were) and that they have a constitution that is markedly different from our own. But there was no hard and fast definition as to what they actually were. They were considered to be extremely powerful.

Wadi Rum

In the southeastern corner of the kingdom of Jordan lies Wadi Rum, a great granite elevation that rises out of the desert in a spectacular manner. The name is said to mean "high" or "elevated," and refers to what is certainly a spectacular geological phenomenon. According to legend, however, the feature is what remains of a city that was built by the djinn, which was their home in prehistoric times. This was allegedly the city of Iblis from which the demon ruled the surrounding lands and from which the djinn went out to do his bidding. In the end, says the legend, Allah could stand such blasphemy no longer; he defeated Iblis and turned his city to stone. Even so Wadi Rum is still associated with magic and great powers, and, some will say, the djinn are still supposed to lodge somewhere among its crags and still venture out into the surrounding deserts—maybe to attack passing travelers with their awesome powers. The local *fugara* (Bedouin witch doctors) still regard it with deep suspicion and state that it is the abode of demons that often swarm invisibly from it. Indeed, so strong was the connection that many have suggested that H.P. Lovecraft may have used Wadi Rum as the model for his Irem the Accursed, the Lost City of Pillars, and home of terrible prehuman forces. It was believed that the djinn were skilled architects and builders and that King Solomon (the only mortal ever to subdue them) used their powers to build his Temple at Jerusalem.

Dark Fairies

In ancient Bedouin lore there is reputedly a set of ancient texts collectively known as *The Book of the Gateway*, which are attributed to the *Muqarribun* (the ghost priests of Southern Jordan) and which make reference to the djinn and to their city at Wadi Rum. For the Muqarribun the granite outcrop was a place of immense power and the gateway to another world, through which djinn swarmed like locusts—invisible to most eyes in our world (only the Muqarribun themselves could see them), but certainly able to do great evil if they so chose. The Muqarribun considered themselves as exorcists, and the *Book of the Gateway* partly consists of a number of texts for driving these creatures away. Even then, they will simply return to the rocks where they live and await a fresh chance to wreak mischief or evil. The djinn were, said the Muqarribun in their text, creatures of air, formed from the "end of the fire," of "smokeless smoke." By this it is assumed that they were creatures of the air, perhaps made from floating dust and pure light.

The djinn were also often associated with the dead; across counties such as Iraq and Iran, they were supposed to haunt abandoned grave-yards sometimes in the shape of feral dogs and jackals, but sometimes in the forms of mist and smoke, which hung over these cemeteries like a shroud. As the dead usually hated the living and were continu-ally seeking a way back into the physical world, they were often hos-tile toward Mankind. They would seek to possess those who either crossed or ventured too close to the cemeteries in which they dwelt, and would then use the physical bodies to hurt or even kill others.

Brollaghan

The swarming djinn emanating from Wadi Rum or some long-abandoned graveyard contains echoes of the fairies swarming from ancient mounds and raths in Ireland; from hillsides in Scotland, and from old ruins, groves, and forts in England and France. And similar to the djinn, there were creatures in the fairy world that seemed to be made of air and smoke or of other natural elements. One of these was the brollaghan, a fairy crea-ture that appears in Scottish lore—particularly that associated with the Highlands—which seemed to be composed of little more than fog and woodsmoke. According to tradition, it seemed to be found in low-lying and marshy places or on open heathland. Despite being something of a smoky creature, the brollaghan can take on a more substantive shape, especially one that is reasonably well-known to the viewer. In this way it tries to lure the unfortunate and unwary wayfarer into dangerous places such as bogs and cliff edges from which he or she cannot readily be extricated. Why the fairy should chose to do this is unknown, but it seems to have a dislike of humans. This is probably, because, say the legends, being a creature of smoke and swirling dust, it cannot take on a corporeal form (only the appearance of such), and therefore cannot enjoy some of the things that are available to humans.

Far Liath

Although there is no real origin given for the brollaghan, it may be related to the Irish Far (Fear) Liath (the Grey Man), which is often found around the coasts of Northern Ireland (particularly in North Antrim) and around the Western Isles. This is a being that is composed entirely of the fogs that roll in from the sea, and it may take the form of a gigantic humanoid striding shoreward from the ocean. Indeed, in the cliffs outside the North Antrim town of Ballycastle, there is a gap with a stone bridge across it known as the Grey Man's Path, which some locals tend to avoid whenever the weather is poor and there is fog around. If anyone crosses the stone bridge, which is no more than a flat stone across a chasm, when the Grey Man is around, the fairy will spring down and throw its grey cloak around them, blotting everything out, making them miss their step, and fall to their doom in the chasm below.

Boats out at sea were also wary of the Far Liath, as the malevolent fairy represented the thick, clinging fogs that shrouded their positions and sometimes drove them onto the jagged coastal rocks or treacherous reefs out at sea. Before sailing from port, many fishing boat crews offered up a prayer that they would be delivered from the clutch of the Grey Man. And there were also those who took certain precautions: A silver coin that had been all through a church service might be built into the prow of a small boat to keep the Grey Man at bay. A handful of soil blessed by a priest would do the same. But the Grey Man also made his presence known on land. For example, foodstuffs such as potatoes left outside could be turned to rot by the fetid touch of his grey cloak. Good clothes, left on a washing line as he passed by, would be irreparably damaged and would remain dank and cold—a hint of continual dampness—ever after. This was true of the brollaghan too, for when that entity touched food that had been left out it acquired an unpleasant smoky taste and was virtually inedible. Only the act of sprinkling the food with holy water and/or saying a prayer over it would preserve it from the ghastly touch. And these two entities, the brollaghan and the Far Liath, only appeared at certain times of the year—mostly at the end of autumn as winter began to draw in and the air was dank and heavy in both Ireland and Scotland.

In fact, both the Brollaghan and the Far Liath might simply be seen as the embodiments of natural forces—smoke and fog—and in keeping to some extent with the origin of the fairy idea within the natural world. Both of them created trouble for individuals in their own right. They were, however, what Yeats has described as "solitary fairies," only appearing at certain times of the year and in certain atmospheric conditions. But it was the trooping and swarming fairies that were probably most feared within the rural communities of Western Europe. Similar to the Macara Shee, the Fairy Cavalcade that traveled along the roads, it was widely believed that fairies left their forts and mounds and traveled widely abroad, sometimes creating mayhem and havoc as they did so. These were simply referred to in Scotland as "the Sluagh" meaning "the host." There is no real description of them except that some tales simply refer to them as having "wings like crows or eagles" (hardly the delicate butterfly wings of Walt Disney!). On these they traveled from one place to another, even to far distant countries where they held parties and made merry. In other versions, they created great windstorms to bear them aloft and to carry them along. As they traveled they often gave an almighty cry that became known in the Highlands as "sluagh gan" (or, "the cry of the Host," and this has given us our English word *slogan* as used in, say, the advertising industry or in political electioneering.

Sluaghs

Like the djinn who were associated with sandstorms in the deserts and like the Semitic seraphim and cherubim who were associated with thunder and lightning (symbols of Yahweh's power and anger), the Sluagh were connected to changes in atmospheric conditions. Great winds carried them here and there and the passing of such a storm often heralded their presence and was a thing to be feared. From such conditions the Sluagh might drop down and make mischief among humans on the ground below. For example, they might fire stones or "elf bolts" (small stone-like objects) at both humans and animals in the fields. A blow from either of these was quite painful—a chance blow might even kill.

During the 1832–33 Land Census commissioned by the Duke of Wellington's government, solders in the Magilligan and Dungiven areas of North Derry interviewed several people who claimed to have been hit by missiles mischievously thrown from "fairy clouds" (the passing Sluagh) with the intent of doing harm.

An old woman, living at Gelvin near Dungiven (close to an ancient fairy fort) in 1832 showed the Census Investigator—a member of the Royal Engineers who conducted the land survey and who recorded a number of incidents in the area—a purple mark on her thigh, which she claimed was the result of a blow from a fairy bolt that had been fired by the Sluagh as they passed in a cloud. She had, she said, been drawing water from a well when a strong wind had come upon her. The Slaugh had probably taken exception to her using the well and had fired a bolt as they passed, hitting her high on the leg. Her daughter, who lived with her, showed the investigator a similar mark on her arm, which she also said had come from a stone or fairy bolt. She had been tending cattle in a field near the fort, and as the Sluagh passed they fired bolts at the cattle for sport, one of which had struck her on the arm. Though she was wearing a thick woollen jacket, the force of the blow had left its mark through the material. A number of farmers also told stories of cattle and sheep in the mountains that had actually been killed or badly injured by fairy bolts.

Dark Fairies

The fairy fort at Gelvin and its flying hordes appears in a number of other stories from the Dungiven area, including one told by a renowned storyteller, Denis McCready, at the end of the 19th century, concerning a weaver named Joseph McPhearson who dwelt in a house close by. Each night he was tormented by the partying as the fairies came and went from the fort on their nocturnal flights. Indeed, on their journeys they even invaded his house, causing a mess and wreckage all around. In desperation McPhearson and his wife brought in a Protestant clergyman who tried to exorcise the crowd. The fairies, however, made a mockery of him and rejected his ritual. In the end the weaver was forced to strike a tragic deal with them, promising them the life of his next born child in return for peace and quiet. Both McPhearson and his wife were quite old and it was expected that the bargain would never be claimed. All the same, his wife did give birth and the baby was claimed and slain by the fairies. Eventually Joseph McPhearson and his wife left the Gelvin area and took passage on a ship to America, never to return. Remnants of the fairy fort at Gelvin can, however, still be seen, and to some extent are still regarded with a mixture of fear and suspicion by some locals.

In his book *Witchcraft and Folklore of the West of Scotland*, published in 1851, Robert McKay records a story from the Cowal Peninsula concerning a man named McAllister from the Isle of Bute, who was attacked by the Sluaghs. He had grazed his sheep on the mountainside close to a deep and extremely dark cave, which was supposed to be the Sluagh's abode. When several of his best animals had been found dead—supposedly killed by fairy bolts and stones—he had gone to the cave mouth to remonstrate with the fairies and to demand some form of compensation for his loss. No sooner had he opened his mouth to speak when the Sluagh swarmed out of the cave in a cloud accompanied by a fierce wind. They seem to have been tiny creatures, no bigger than bees, but the air was filled with the sound of their whirring wings. They pummelled McAllister and fired stones and bolts and beat him brutally with sticks until he was covered in scars and bruises. They drove him back down the mountain, tripping him up as he went and adding to his misery. Even when he returned home they would not leave him be, but followed him to his house, firing bolts and hurling

stones at the windows and seeking to enter, perhaps to torment him further. In the end, like the unfortunate Joseph McPhearson, McAllister was forced to leave the area for good. The Sluagh were not beings to be trifled with.

But it was not only physical injury for which the Sluagh were famed and feared. As the cloud of fairies passed by human habitations, they tended to gather things up and take them with them wherever they happened to be going, whether it be back to their forts or to some other place (usually a foreign country). They would lift property and livestock without hesitation, and sometimes even humans, particularly human children who had been left unguarded and unprotected in their cribs. Thus, items and people who went missing were said to have been swept up by the Sluagh and carried off in a "fairy wind."

For many farmers in both Scotland and Ireland, livestock was a special issue, for it was thought that the fairies were especially attracted to cattle and sheep, which they carried off to eat in the banqueting halls beneath their earthen forts. Sometimes, however, they would leave one of their own behind in place of the captured animal—an old and sickly fairy who would take on the guise of a cow. Thus, a formerly healthy animal would become thin and sickly and would eventually die. This idea would form the basis of the Scottish folktale, *The Laird of Gesto*, which comes from both the Isle of Skye and from Benbecula in Uist. Here, the Sluagh was known by a number of names, such as the Spirit Multitude or the Na Fir Chis (the Nimble Men), and were supposed to have been ancient Celtic gods who were banished to the sky with the coming of Christianity to become the Merry Dancers who formed the basis of the aurora borealis, which could be seen in the northern skies from time to time.

In the story, the Laird and a servant set out from Gesto in Skye to visit a kinsman in Benbecula. They travel by boat, which they take to the Eubhadh Port Channel and then set out on foot overland. They have not been walking long when they are overtaken by a fierce windstorm and foul weather and are forced to seek shelter. High up on a hillside they find a broch (a house or fort made from sods) and knock on the door for admission. They are brought in to the fire by an old man and his many sons who appear to live there. Under the ancient laws of Highland hospitality, their host is compelled to offer them something to eat, but there is nothing in the house. He now sends several of his sons out into the foul weather to see if they can find some food for their guests. It is only then that the Laird sees that some of the "sons" have wings under their shirts and he realizes that he and his servant are among the Sluagh who have tormented the Western Isles for some time. However, he says nothing.

The Sluagh return with a cow for the spit, which the Laird recognizes as one of his own. The "sons" say that they were passing over Skye and, in Gesto, they found a milkmaid milking a cow. As she worked, one of the animals lifted its hoof and kicked her, sending her flying. Rising, she cursed the cow and this gave the Sluagh the opportunity to sweep down and take it and claim it as their own. However, so that it would not be missed, they left one of their own in its place, a fairy that was old and dead. This is the story that the "sons" tell the old man, who puts the cow on the spit and offers it to his guest. The Laird and his servant both eat and pass the night quite pleasantly with the Sluagh. In the morning, however, the Laird decides to cancel his trip to Benbecula and return to Gesto; when he arrives home, he finds the place in an uproar. The entire household is on the very point of death. The Laird's favorite cow had died the night before, and the maids had cooked and eaten it under the impression that it was a real cow. All had badly sickened afterward. The Laird calls the dairymaid who had been milking the animal and had subsequently cursed it. He reveals that he knows what she has done and, although she is astonished, she admits her curse. The Laird then reveals that what they have eaten is an old dead fairy man in the guise of a cow, and that his tainted flesh is what has poisoned them all. Through herbs and potions he manages to heal all the servants, but in the end dismisses the dairymaid.

Cattle were continually being carried off by the Sluagh and were sometimes found wandering many miles away from their original fields. Skeptics might say that they had wandered there by themselves, but the fairies provided a ready explanation for the distances that were sometimes involved. Sometimes other animals were taken too such as sheep and hens, and once again the notion of fairy abduction served to satisfy queries as to why they were sometimes found wandering so far from their original places. Bits and pieces of property were lifted as well, sometimes carried away by fierce winds. Posts and bits of buildings, boxes, chests, and other items that had been left outside were all taken, and if the owner was lucky they were dumped elsewhere. Many items were never seen again and were supposed to be held in fairy halls. This might have been due to natural elements, but the suspicion of fairy involvement was always there.

And people were also swept up by the raging winds. Children left unprotected in their cribs to sleep in the sunshine by the doors to cottages were particularly at risk. A sudden windstorm might spring up as the fairy host passed and the infant would suddenly disappear, carried off by the vanishing throng. If the child happened to be unbaptized, then it was especially at risk. The only way to protect it was to leave a crucifix or holy medal in the crib beside it, or for an adult (usually the child's father) to throw an item of clothing over it as it slept to mark it as a human child. Then no fairy could touch it. In some cases, however, as we shall see later, the fairies might leave one of their own in its place—an old, sickly being—as they did with the cow in the tale of the Laird of Gesto, but this occurs rather infrequently. Even if a baptized child were in the house it could still be stolen by the Sluagh. Of all the fairy hosts it was said that the Flying Host had the most disregard of priestly protections. However, there were precautions against them: A child should never be left to sleep opposite a west-facing window, because it was usually from the west that the Sluagh came; iron tongs from the fire should be placed across the blanket of the crib because, like most fairies, the Sluagh feared iron; failing all of this, a lock of hair, taken from the head of either parent would protect the sleeping infant (this may have had the same origin as the item of clothing it marked the infant as a human child). In some cases, the child might be found many miles away (even in some cases in another country), or else might be discovered accidentally living elsewhere, or might even turn up at his or her former home many years later. In many cases, they were changed in some way (for example, their wits might be gone) through their involvement in the fairy world and through prolonged contact with "the Other Sort."

It was not only small children or babies who might get carried away by "the fairy wind"—grown people might be taken by the Sluagh as well. There are tales from Ireland, Scotland, and Wales of people being lifted off their feet and carried over the fields to some other place by swarming fairies. Sometimes they are invited to partake in the fairy revelries in some other location, and sometimes they are just dumped and abandoned as the fairies troop on somewhere else. A story known as *The Trip to London*, which comes from the area of Craig—between Toberkeigh and Dunseverick in North Antrim, Ireland—combines elements of both the Irish and Scots traditions and tells of a laboring man who was carried off by the Sluagh across the Irish Sea. His name, according to the story, was Thomas McCaughan (which is a fairly common name in that area), and he lived close to Toberkeigh (the blind well). In the fields across from his house, between Ballyloughbeg and Straidbilly, was an old earthen rath that lay close to the roadside. It was a dark and gloomy place with queer broken shadows about it even on the brightest days, and it was generally regarded as a fairy place by people round about. The story says that Tom McCaughan was cursed with great curiosity, and it was that which proved his undoing. One evening he stepped out of his cottage to take the evening air on a rather bright moonlit night around Halloween. He walked up to the top of his yard and looked down over the fields toward the rath. In the twilight it seemed to be all lit up and there seemed to be people coming and going from it. Anxious to see what was going on, he climbed over a gate and made his way down across the field towards the rath. His presence seemed to alert the fairies who were within it and they rose in a swarm out of the earthen walls and swept toward him, like hundreds of angry bees. A wind seemed to gather around him and it blew so strongly that it started to lift him off his feet and carry him aloft. All around him he could hear the angry and complaining voices of the fairies as they bore him up higher and higher until the fields had fallen away below him. It carried him over the houses of Dunseverick village, out over the harbor, and far out into the wild North Atlantic. He was carried on and on, and although the fairies muttered and fumed around him he found that he could not open his mouth to answer them. Soon he saw the coast of England coming up, and as they crossed it, the wind began to slow slightly, for it is believed that the Irish Sluagh only have a fraction of their power on English soil. Soon, far below, he saw the lights of a great city, which they seemed to be passing over. But all the while he seemed to be dropping as the Irish fairies began to lose their power. Then it suddenly ceased and he fell like a stone into the streets of the city below, fortunately landing on some bags that had been piled up in a back alley. He lay there for a while realizing that he'd been dumped in a foreign city without even so much as a penny to bless himself.

The city that he'd been taken to was London and it was a fine place, but only if you had plenty of money. Tom McCaughan was poor and he knew nobody that could lend him some cash in order to get a boat fare home. He had to look out for jobs and take what he could get. He worked as a builder, a cook and a porter in hotels, and a street-cleaner in the early morning. He took the meanest and cheapest lodgings he could get. He kept to himself and any penny he didn't spend on rent or on feeding himself he put away toward his trip back home to Ireland.

Tom McCaughan lived in London for two years, and at the end of that time, through his careful saving, he had enough money gathered together for his boat fare home and a little bit more. All the time that he'd been in England, he'd never forgotten his wife and daughter back in Toberkeigh, and he'd missed them greatly. He wanted to bring them back something, a present from his time in England. He had a bit of money left over after he paid the fare, so he went to one of the big stores in the city and bought a dress for his daughter and a shawl for his wife, both of which he wrapped in separate parcels. Then, putting the presents under his arm, he set out for the boat to Ireland.

As he reached the quay, he paused by the entrance to a side street close to the docks. There a wind seemed to be swirling and blowing, although the day seemed very calm, lifting bits and pieces of paper and rubbish and whirling them around. It all looked very strange and Tom McCaughan's curiosity got the better of him once more; he went to investigate it. The wind caught the tails of his coat and was so strong that it began to lift him again. He was poked and prodded, and there were more mutterings in his ear. The wind lifted him, parcels and all, and carried him up into the sky over the city. Soon the English countryside was laid out below him and he was being carried along toward the coast once more. Then he was over the sea and heading toward Ireland, and in the dark below he could see the lights of ships coming and going. He traveled in the wind all night, being kicked and thumped by invisible beings round about. As morning came, the wind picked up speed, but he began to descend toward the Irish coast. Below him he saw the house of Dunseverick and he began to realize that it was the Sluagh from his own area that had gathered him up; they were heading home, back to the earthen fort near his house.

Suddenly the wind stopped and he found himself falling toward his fields in Craig, landing on a bag of lime, which somebody had left beside a bush. The murmurings and mutterings were gone, as the Sluagh disappeared into the old rath once more. Dusting himself off Tom McCaughan made his way up to the house, still holding tight to the parcels in which he had the presents for his wife and daughter. As he walked into his cottage he found the two women at work, his daughter making bread, and his wife sewing bits of material, just as they had been doing on the night that the fairies had carried him off to London. However, when he came in, neither of the women looked up or even took the slightest notice of him, but carried on with their sewing. Indignant, Tom McCaughan expressed the opinion that this was indeed a fine welcome home after being away for so long, he said. His daughter looked up from her bread-making and laughed. She told him that far from being away for two years, he'd only been gone from the house for two minutes! In an attempt to prove what he said, McCaughan open the presents that he had bought from the big London store, but each parcel contained only a handful of horse-dung. Once more, to prove his point, he tried to show them the money that he'd earned in London, which he was going to use for his fare home, but when he opened his pockets they too were full of dung mixed with leaves and acorns. Nevertheless, he knew he had been confounded by the Sluagh because of his curiosity about the old rath. He never got over the experience and died shortly afterward from a mysterious illness. The story of his abduction, however, was told in the Toberkeigh area for many years after his death as a warning of meddling with the Sluagh. It was recorded as told by his own grandson who lived in the area.

The story showed another often significant element in the dealings between humans and fairies such as the Sluagh—that is the manipulation of the perception of time. In the tale, Tom McCaughan was certain that he had been away in London for two years—indeed, he had lived at various addresses there—whereas according to his wife and daughter, he had only been gone for two minutes. In some way, the Sluagh had managed to alter the passage of time. This was, as we shall see later, a feature of those who had been carried off by the fairies in general, and by the Sluagh in particular. However, it usually worked the other way. Some people were lifted by the trooping fairies and carried away for what they thought was at best a few hours or at worst a night, only to return home after the experience to find that many years (even as much as a hundred) had passed. This was often put down to "fairy magic."

Fairy Wind

If a "fairy wind" passed by, there were certain protections that might be taken to safeguard the individual. One might, for example, say the words "God bless me" and genuflect, which had the effect of driving off most of the fairy kind, because few fairies could withstand the Holy Name (although in some stories this was not infallible). One might also carry a piece of wood into which the form of a cross had been inscribed (this was also useful for warding off witches, as well as for knocking fairies off course). When traveling, it was wise to keep a page torn from or containing several verses from the Bible inside one's hat or shoe, or, failing that, something made of pure iron about one's person. This would keep one safe from fairies and evil things in general, but would also guard against the Sluagh. One last defense was to urn one's coat inside out and to repeat the following incantation: "My face from you, my back to you." This would serve to confuse the Sluagh and they would pass by without seeing their potential victim. However, it should be stressed that none of these defenses were completely failsafe, and the individual might be taken in any case.

When traveling it was wise to avoid bridges and crossroads, because these were the inevitable haunts of the Sluagh and all sorts of supernatural creatures. However, it was here that most travelers were thought to be taken by the host of the air. Crossroads, of course, had a sinister history, because this was a point where many ways crossed, but bridges joined one part of road to another, perhaps spanning a river or ravine, and therefore those who crossed were particularly susceptible to the attentions of the fairy host. In places such as Brittany and the Isle of Man bridges were regarded with suspicion, and those who crossed them without the proper protection would be liable to get swept away by the fairy host. It was therefore wise in these locations to say "Good morning" and "By your leave" before crossing the bridge in order to ensure reaching the other side.

Fairy Funerals

Nor were the trooping fairies only interested in the living; they also had a strong connection with the dead. In parts of Ireland and Scotland they were known as the Sluagh-na-Marbh, which emphasized this connection. Some tales recount how fairies claimed bodies that were being laid out for burial—before the final rites were completed—and then reanimated them in some way, turning them into *marbh bheo* (nightwalking dead), which the fairies then used to terrify the corpse's former neighbors. So strong was this belief that in parts of the Western Isles and Scotland the bier upon which the corpse or coffin had been carried to the grave was ritually broken by a priest or clergyman after the funeral. This was to stop it from falling into the hands of the Sluagh, who might then use it to summon the corpse from the grave and turn it into a kind of zombies or vampire-like creature. Once again, it was unwise to leave a corpse lying close to a west-facing window, because this was a clear invitation to the Sluagh to enter and use it for their own means. It was good to say the final rites and take the body from the house and to consecrated ground (on which, according to some traditions, the fairies had no power) as quickly as possible.

This connection with the dead may well have stemmed from an ancient Celtic belief common in a number of counties: On certain nights of the year the fairies, under God's command, were compelled to escort the souls of all those who had died within the previous year to the Gates of Paradise, a place which they themselves, having no souls, were not permitted to enter. This "fairy funeral" (as it was called) either took place in a procession along the nightbound country roads, or else with the Sluagh through the air. Those who witnessed it were in special danger, for the fairy kind had the power to sweep them away along with the wailing souls and carry them with the host into the Afterlife. According to conventional wisdom throughout Ireland and Scotland, it was wiser to stay indoors at such times of the year.

Wales, too, had its stories of such an aerial procession. Here the fairies were sometimes led by a phenomenon known as the *canwll corfe* (corpse candle). This was a strange and eerie light akin to the flame of a flickering candle, which was seen from time to time in ancient graveyards or high in the night sky, and was said to presage death in a community. It either led the souls of the dead or the fairies to their Eternal Reward, or, according to some, to the realm of the fairies, who sometimes laid claim to the spirits of the wicked.

This, of course, introduces another element: Those who died without confessing their sins or after having lived a particularly wicked life might not see either Heaven or Hell, but rather became the property of the fairies who took them to their own world and made them their slaves. In some tales from the Western Isles of Scotland, the Sluagh had the power to do this, and so it was essential to make one's peace with the Church before death. Those who dealt in "the Black Airts" (witchcraft) and other secretive sins might expect to be taken by the Sluagh at the moment of death and before any religious funerary service (which might save them).

This notion that a host of supernatural beings were waiting to snatch away an unforgiven soul at the point of death seems to have crossed the Atlantic Ocean into Puritan New England. In the remoter areas of rural Rhode Island and in parts of Massachusetts, there was a belief (perhaps still current even today) that harmful spirits, sometimes in the disguise of jackdaws or whippoorwills, clustered in the trees around the house of a very evil person who was close to death. When the person died the birds flocked down in order to try to catch the departing soul before it left the house (and the physical world). If the birds continued to wait and cry for a long time after the death, they had missed the spirit, but if they suddenly fell silent, the soul of the evil person was theirs. So prevalent was the superstition that it appears in several stories by the horror and fantasy writer H.P. Lovecraft. The thronging birds, of course, may correspond to the Celtic Sluagh, seeking to gain the souls of the dead for their own purposes. Indeed, in some forms of Scottish folklore—and by extension American—the Sluagh are in fact the horde of the unforgiven dead, flying through the air, denied entrance to either Heaven or Hell. Although they sometimes performed good acts—such as rescuing animals or humans from high places where they had become trapped—they were usually hostile toward the living and sought to do them harm.

The Sluagh, however, were not the only groups of fairies to travel through the air. In some ancient tales—including Irish, Welsh, and English—the fairy courts of local fairy rulers would sometimes rise up and travel from one place to another, echoing the peripatetic courts of some medieval rulers. These courts were set up in various places— ancient standing stones, ruined buildings, even decaying Christian symbols such as old stone crosses—before moving on to the next location. At a place known as Tamlaghtard (the High Plague Marker) on the Magilligan coast in North Derry, Ireland, the fairy court was supposed to meet on a high headland before trooping on through the air to meet again at a spot further along the shoreline (or into the Western Isles, which are easily seen on a good day from Tamlaghtard), and this was typical of many such beliefs. Indeed, the court of Oberon in Shakespeare's play *A Midsummer Night's Dream* seems to have the same sort of quality about it. Puck, for example (the name is suggestive of Pook or the Celtic Puca, suggesting a nature or air spirit), who is a member of that court, states that he "walks up and down" the world, and it is possible that the court itself moved with him, in the manner of natural spirits or sprites. The idea of the traveling localized fairy "king" and his court were often paramount in much of English folklore, which is possibly from where Shakespeare drew much of his inspiration for *A Midsummer Night's Dream.*

Fairy Courts

In Scotland, however, such traveling courts and fairy gatherings took on a much more sinister tone. Here, they were sometimes known as the Unseelie Court. The term seelie (meaning blessed or holy, and referring to gatherings of more beneficial fairies) has its root in the old Germanic word *selig* or, in Old English, *saelig* meaning "harmless" (which has given us our English word *silly*—that is, foolish harmlessness). There was nothing harmless, however, about the Unseelie Court. This was a gathering of dark fairies, some of whom were even misshapen and inhuman in form, who behaved very much in the manner of the Sluagh. Their only purpose seemed to be to plot and carry out ways to harm or disadvantage humans in the area where they gathered. They carried away livestock or made them fall ill, they threw stones and elf bolts, they stole items from nearby houses, they injured children and adults, they damaged property, and they brought general ill-luck to an area. They appeared to travelers on the roads, usually after dark, and carried them off on what became known as the Hell-Ride—a dangerous ride through the air through bushes, bracken, and rocks. Or they would beat travelers with sticks until they were badly cut and bruised.

In parts of the Celtic world, the court gathered under the malign auspices of a Grand Master or sometimes a dark local fairy king who was equated in many respects with the Devil. He presided over the activities and gave the fairies their orders for the night—for example, whom to harm, whom to terrify, whom to work evil magics against, and so on. In many respects, the Unseelie Court had all the attributes of the popular conception of a Witches' Sabbat. In parts of France—particularly in places such as the Jura region or in parts of Brittany, there were similar gatherings, although these were known as *Precieuses*—a name taken from the grand salons of Paris where fashionable ladies would gather to make witty but disparaging comments about people they knew or were in the public eye. The name was taken from the French word *preciosite* meaning "precious" (in a derogatory way), which was said to reflect the nature of these ladies. The cattiness and spite that characterized such gatherings may have been transferred into the nature of these fairy assemblies.

Dark Fairies

Similar to the Sluagh in Scotland and Ireland, such fairies were believed to be spiteful and malicious, always ready to do humans an ill turn; contact with them was to be rigorously avoided. This was not always easy, for such gatherings were often close to public thoroughfares or even to human habitations. Crossroads were a particular favorite throughout Brittany. The ghastly host would suddenly descend on a lonely rural place where roads crossed each other (a sign of great and dark magic in itself) to await travelers. When they had fulfilled whatever evil purpose they had intended, they would rise again like birds and travel on to work their devilry somewhere else. No one was safe from them unless he or she carried a piece of iron, a holy medal blessed by a priest or bishop, or a silver coin that had been all the way through a Church service, and so it was imbued with holy power. Even with all these protections, the traveler might still not be completely safe from the attentions of the *precieuses*. Once again, it was better to stay indoors at night just in case such creatures were abroad and lurking in the rural darkness.

In Scotland, a number of tales are told about the Unseelie Court and of those who have encountered it. One concerns a traveler journeying on the Isle of Barra from Brevig to Craigstone at a bad time of the year when the fairies were very active. The man's name was Andrew MacPhearson, and he did some work for the priest, Father John MacDonald, who was the clergyman on the Island. Father John was a severe and stern man, and he often spoke out against the fairies and the Black Airt, but he and Andrew got on well enough.

This night Andrew was going to Craigstone to see his sister, who was ill. He had reached a place on the road called Taigh an Ghearraidh Mhoir (the house of the big wall) when he heard a strange disturbance in the air—a kind of muttering and noises like distant shouting. There was a bit of a wind picking up as well, whirling and dancing among the rocks. Looking out across the countryside he thought he saw a number of people sitting away in a hollow in the land off to his right. He couldn't make out who they were but at a distance he thought that it might be some of his neighbors; he was about to shout when something distracted him and he looked away. When he looked back, the hollow seemed empty and all he saw was moonlight and shadows. Thinking that his eyes were playing tricks, he walked on.

Then on the wind came a whisper behind him, saying, *Andrew MacPhearson*. He turned and there was no one there. Now thinking that his ears were playing tricks, he ignored it, but the whisper came again, low and husky on the breeze: *Andrew McPhearson*. And then he knew it was the fairies and that they were on the road behind him, in the air, or among the roadside stones, and so he quickened his pace. Behind him, the wind seemed to gather. *Priest's servant!* The whisper came again, but seemingly with more venom this time, and the wind began to pull at the ends of his trousers as if to trip him up. He quickened his step even more and the wind seemed to pull at him, obstructing him as he tried to walk.

"Leave me alone!" he shouted, although he was unsure to whom he shouted it, for there was nobody near him. He reached a turn of the road, and as he went around the corner, the wind caught him and lifted him off his feet entirely. It carried him into the fields, over rocks and stones, and down into a hollow in the land. There was a group of shadows, huddled around as if sitting on various stones. Andrew MacPhearson was terrified, because some of the shapes in front of him did not look completely human and he knew where he might be—in the Unseelie Court.

Come forward Andrew MacPhearson. The voice was like the hiss of a snake, but it carried an authoritative tone. He knew that, though his legs were shaking, he could not refuse the summons. The voice seemed to come from a great shadow that seemed to have the head of a dark horse, and it was seated on the highest stone, leaning forward toward him. The creatures around its feet seemed to be smaller and much more misshapen, gnarled like the roots or branches of trees, but the only thing that could really be made out was the dull yellow glow of their eyes. The great shadow spoke again. *Come forward, servant of a priest!* A shadowy claw-like hand was stretched out with its index finger pointing directly at him. Swallowing loudly and nervously, Andrew stepped forward.

You are the servant of a priest, Andrew MacPhearson—a priest that has denounced our kind from the pulpit for many's a year. He has turned the thoughts of the people against our kind—in the olden days they used to worship us and leave gifts for us, but no more. And all because of this priest—Father John MacDonald. You have tended both his house and garden for him, and while our powers cannot touch him because of his holy office, we adjudge that you take the weight of the responsibility for these things upon your shoulders and receive whatever punishment should be meted out to the troublesome priest.

Andrew MacPhearson was aghast. "But I am no priest," he protested. "I am only a humble and honest laboring man. I have always lived a good and honest life, and I'm well thought of amongst my neighbours. Why should I take the spiteful anger of your kind that is due to Father MacDonald?" The dark finger that pointed at him never wavered, but the horse-like head seemed to move slightly and there was a kind of stirring among the other shadows around the rocks.

Because you have been close to him—been his servant—you have the stink of a priest about you, the creature answered. *To us, you are as good as any priest. You will take the weight of our condemnation, for this is the judgment of the Unseelie Court. Let it be so!* And with that the wind arose once more and the beings around the bases of the great rocks gathered up stones and began to pelt him. They lifted sticks and beat him about the legs and body, and as the wind grew stronger he was lifted up, rising higher and higher above the Island. What money he had in his pockets fell from them to the ground below. He was whisked along in the mighty wind with the nightbound country passing below him, and all the while he was being beaten with sticks and pelted with stones and elfshot. Higher and higher, he was carried until he couldn't even see the lights of the houses in the countryside far below.

"In the Name of God!" he cried. "Are you going to carry me all the way up to the gates of Heaven itself?" At the mention of the Holy Name, the wind suddenly dropped and Andrew MacPhearson fell like a stone through the darkness of the night, landing on a pile of hay in the comer of a large yard.

Dusting himself off, he got up and looked around him. Although badly bruised from the beating and his fall, he was pretty much unhurt, but he had no idea where he might be. Because he could hear the sea, he reckoned he was somewhere near the coast, which is where he found himself when the sun at last came up. He spent a day walking along an unfamiliar shore, and when he eventually came to a small cluster of houses near sunset he found himself to be near Tarbert in the Mull of Kintyre, many miles away across the sea from his home in Barra. The people there were kind and took him in, giving him shelter and looking after him in his piteous condition, but they had no way of getting him home. So he had to live with them for several months before a fishing boat bound for the Northern Isles called into port and was able to give him a lift. Even then he had to make his way across the islands back to Barra and this took him more than a week.

Tired and footsore, he arrived home to find that his sister's condition had worsened in the time he was away and that she had died. He had just arrived back in time for her funeral. Many of his neighbors thought that he himself was dead—perhaps drowned in a fall, and their grief at the death of his sister was lightened by the joy of his return. As soon as the funeral was over, Andrew went straight to Father MacDonald and told him what had happened. The priest took it all very seriously and made the sign of the cross over him in case he still had the touch of fairy magic about him. After that Andrew seldom ventured far from his own house and he had no further encounters with the Unseelie Court. They had attacked him because he was the servant of a priest and they were greatly opposed to anything that had to do with the Church or clergymen.

In many respects the tales of the Unseelie Court often closely parallel those concerning the Sluagh. Indeed, in some parts of Scotland, the two are interchangeable, although in some of them the court has the power to place terrible afflictions on some of those who cross them. For example, they can cause a hump to grow on their backs, their mouths to be stopped, or their feet to be turned around so that they ended up walking backward and away from the direction that they wished to go. And this they did out of pure spite. Small wonder then that people kept to their houses at night for fear of meeting with them in some lonely place!

For many cultures, the air was full of spirits—whether it be the fallen angels of the Semitic tradition, the swarming djinn in places such as the Wadi Rum, or the Sluagh and Unseelie Courts of the Celtic world. Many of these swarms were hostile toward Mankind and were to be avoided, but even if individuals were able to do this, there were still other fairies waiting to trap them and drag them away. These were the fairies who lived under the earth, and who were just as dangerous.

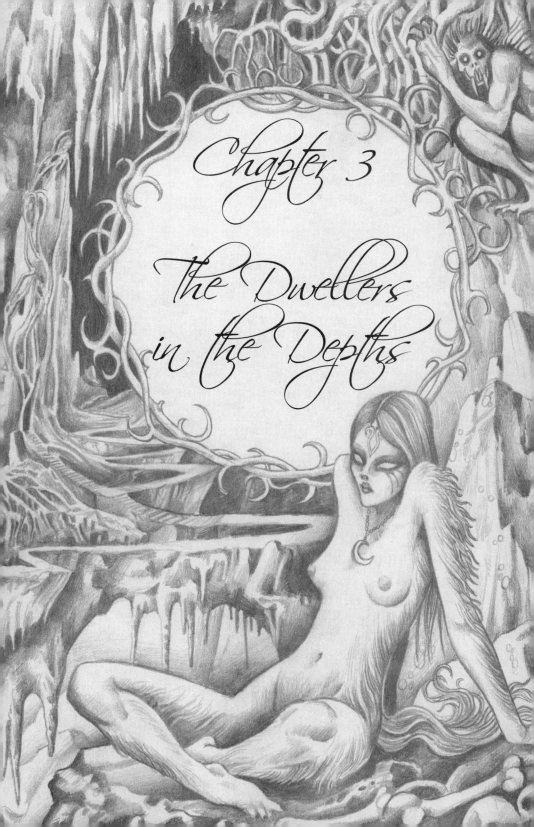

Chapter 3

The Dwellers in the Depths

erhaps from the very earliest times, primitive man has looked into the darkness of great caves, deep ravines, and chasms, and wondered what lay down there. And as he looked, he probably experienced a mixture of curiosity and fear, for whatever lurked down there in the darkness might not be pleasant. Were there monsters concealed by the gloom (some legends say that there are even today), or did another race of people lurk down there, avoiding the sunlight? (This has formed the basis of many science fiction and fantasy stories.) Might something terrible befall our ancestors if they ventured down into the stygian gloom?

These two ideas—of something monstrous or a lost race living beneath the surface of the world—combine to create the idea of underground fairies. The lands underneath the earth were supposedly the abode of demons and fallen angels, creatures who had lost their serene looks and who were ugly and nasty to look at. This was translated into the idea of gnomes, goblins, dwarves, and kobolds. These creatures haunted caves and mines, and their underground existence, away from God's beneficial sunlight, shaped their features and made them hard, mischievous, and cruel. Indeed, the element cobalt, which miners had noticed polluted other elements with which it came in contact, derives its name from the German kobolds and their alleged nefarious activities. And if they were ugly and misshapen beings, as with the Unseelie Court discussed previously, they were bound to be evil. Also, if they lived down in the darkness they were bound to be sly, secretive, and hostile toward those who lived in the sunlight.

The story of races living beneath the ground appears in a number of cultures. Strange tunnels in Brazil and Argentina, for example, were supposedly built by a subterranean race in order to travel to and from the surface, and the lost underground country of Argatha with its capital Shamballah is said to lie somewhere beneath the Himalayas. Even in North Carolina, some of the "balds" (low hills where grass will not grown on the summit, situated on the edge of Great Smokies) are said to be hollow and contain hidden realms in which people may live. There are old Cherokee legends concerning Judaculla, a giant warrior who came to the surface from an underground country, and who left signs of his passing there. Judaculla's Rock can be found in the Caney Fork River Valley in Jackson County, North Carolina, and is a large stone on which mysterious glyphs have been carved. They were supposed to have been cut there by the giant and his people in the language that is spoken in the lands under the earth, and it remains an enigma to this day.

It is not a massive step to take from stories of mysterious races living under the earth to colonies of fairies living there. The mystery and eeriness of deep, dark holes and fissures fit in well with many of the fairy beliefs. It was not hard to believe that small (perhaps malformed) creatures were living in cliffs and mountains away from human civilization. Perhaps some of the earliest of these tales come from the Germanic and Scandinavian traditions, areas where the landscape seemed to suit such beings.

Kobolds

Kobolds, in fact, may be simply an extension of ancient Germanic Pagan gods and nature spirits. The earliest references to them portray them as household and community spirits, protecting homes and settlements akin to the Lares and di Penates spirits. However, a second strand of them appear to live in deep caves and enclosed valleys in wild and mountainous areas. The name may derive from the word *kefewalt* meaning "a spirit which presides over a single room of a building," although it has been argued that it may also be rooted in the Greek *koba'los* meaning "rogue or evil worker." Classic linguists such as Paul Wrexler have suggested the root word is *kobin*, meaning "pigsty." The use of the suffix *alt* is derived from Old High German, and invariably refers to a supernatural being. In the Germanic mountains, such as the Brocken and Hartz areas of northern Germany, the spirit probably presided over a single area, such as a certain valley or slope, becoming something like a *genus loci* (spirit of place). In this respect it

then became something like a defender of the area, violently attacking those who inadvertently wandered into it. In some areas kobolds were associated with specific trees in these locations, maybe growing in a deep, gloomy glen or close to the mouth of a cave. Representations of the kobold, which were sometimes cut from these trees (either as a good luck charm or as a protective talisman for houses) were often thought to contain the very essence of the kobold itself.

Descriptions of the kobold vary. Sometimes it is portrayed as a little man in neat and dapper clothing—something like the traditional Irish tourist variation of a leprechaun—other times it appears more ferocious and fearsome. In every representation, however, the kobold always appears to have a large mouth. This may be because, as some etymologists have suggested, the name of the sprite may come from an old Germanic word meaning to "laugh loudly and heartily" (a kind of belly-laugh). Indeed, in the 17th century, a common expression in parts of what is now Germany was "to laugh like a kobold," meaning to laugh uproariously.

Apart from the large mouths, kobolds are often depicted in art as little, bent old men with wrinkled faces, often dressed in green and red. This is especially true of those kobolds that live in caves and mines, who are sometimes portrayed in crude miner's gear and are sometimes even portrayed as blind. However, others stories describe them as bearded little men no bigger than 2-year-old children with high-pointed red hoods (this seems to be an average size for kobolds, none of whom are very tall). Others describe them as beautiful child-like creatures with angelic faces—the kobold that dwelt in the ruins of Hudemuchlen Castle near Hodenhagen Luneburg in Lower Saxony was described as such—but this may be through a supposed connection with dead children. Their angelic countenance, of course, did not make them any less evil. In fact it was believed by many Germans that kobolds were the spirits of the hostile dead in physical form, and as such many of them lived underground.

In mining areas within parts of Bavaria, kobolds made their presence known by strange sounds and eerie voices, which many miners claimed to have heard while working in the deep chambers. They were also frequently blamed for accidents that occurred there, such as rockfalls and slippages, some of which resulted in loss of life. They were also believed to delude miners by making veins of worthless ores appear valuable. Thus, miners believed that they had struck gold or silver when in fact the ore was useless. Some of these ores might have been poisonous and cause death.

The idea of the mine kobold may have come from an ancient Germanic notion of cave spirits. These were entities who dwelt deep within caves and fissures in the landscape and whose voices could sometimes be heard by those passing by issuing prophesies and instructions from their gloomy abodes. They were never seen, but simply existed as sepulchral voices issuing from the underground. For some these were the spirits of the dead, lodged somewhere in the far underground instead of passing on to whatever Eternal Reward awaited them, forced to share their supernatural knowledge with the living in some manner. In fact, these beings existed within the Celtic world as well, and from time to time communities gathered (as they sometimes did in Germany) to hear what might happen within the coming month and year if the spirit chose to divulge it. Of course, such spirits were often mischievous or downright evil and issued false prognostications, deliberately designed to mislead, confuse, or spread alarm. When men came to mine in such areas the idea of the spirit may well have transferred itself from the subterranean caverns and into the mine workings. For example, the miners working in the German Ruhr or Westphalia mining areas would often hear voices talking, complaining, or even threatening when there seemed to be no one there. This they thought was the voice of a kobold. Such beliefs were passed to miners in other cultures too; for example, it was said that the "knockers" or "Bluecaps" dwelled deep within the tin mines of Cornwall.

Dwarves

Closely allied to the idea of kobolds was that of dwarves. Again, such a belief was in prominent in the Germanic traditions, although the original concept of a dwarf (a small humanoid being) may be taken from Norse folklore where they are known as *dvergar*. They were not unlike humans, just a bit smaller—the medieval Norse Gylfaginning Edda states, "The dwarfs have the likeness of a human although they live in earth and stones." These small beings dwelt underground and had strong associations with the dead. In fact, they looked very much like the dead: pale-skinned and red-eyed, more closely resembling our idea of a vampire than of a fairy. Akin to the original impressions of the kobold, the idea of the dwarf may have suggested that dwarves were the spirits of the dead that were given some sort of physical form. And like the dead, they were rather hostile toward the living, who could enjoy things that they could not. So they lurked in their light-less caverns beneath the hills away from the sunlight (which, much in the same way as vampires, was invariably fatal to them), contriving how to discomfort or even kill the humans on the surface above them. The *dwarrows* and *dweorges* (*wights*) of Old English tradition seem to have functioned in the same way and were just as hostile toward Humankind. Within the early Norse world, dwarves were creatures to be avoided, the symbols of elder gods that once dwelt deep within the earth. They were supposedly skilled craftsmen and worked with metals found in the earth, and in this respect they might be equated with the Norse *Vaettir*, a form of nature spirit. In their earliest incar-nation they are closely associated with a form of elf that traces its origins from nature spirits. Elves, too, were considered to have the characteristics of the dead and were often regarded as hostile toward men. (Indeed, some of the material that was fired at humans by the Sluagh as they passed was often referred to in the Scottish Highlands as *elfshot*—manufactured by the elves in underground caverns.) Early descriptions of dwarves describe them as black elves, emphasising such a connection.

In early Norse tradition dwarves are not actually small at all, but are roughly the height of an average individual. Although they were usually pale skinned, some accounts depict them as rotting, with faces that resembled skulls, once again drawing attention to their links to the dead. They had more in common with the *draugr,* the walking corpse of Northern folklore that lay in small tomb houses, and that rose from time to time in order to wander about, often creating may-hem amongst the living. As time passed, however, the Scandinavian dwarves seemed to grow smaller and more deformed, perhaps em-phasising the steady decay of their bodies.

Dark Fairies

It is only in later Nordic folklore from around the 11th and 12th centuries that dwarves begin to emerge as entities in their own right. Although a few distinctions are made in the early tales, dwarves are almost identical to elves, or are regarded as some form or offshoot of the elfish species or the walking dead. In later legends they appear to be small, old men with long beards working as miners, metal workers, or smiths, far below ground.

They forge mainly weapons, primarily for the gods of later Norse folklore—Wodin, Thor, and so on—and are considered to be extremely wise in the ways of ancient magics. In both the early Celtic and Saxon worlds, those who worked in metals—smiths and swordmakers—were considered to have great and mystical powers, and were often able to imbue the weapons they made with some of their enchantments. This idea transferred itself into the concept of the dwarfish race living under the earth, down in the dark and heat. However, the dwarf smiths are considered to be extremely surly—even toward the gods, and more so toward humans—and should only be approached with extreme caution. They have great skill and great magical powers, it was said, but are incredibly grim with ferociously short tempers. In this period they are quite a long way from Walt Disney's jolly and caring dwarves in the film *Snow White.*

Around the Scandinavian medieval period (13th and 14th centuries) dwarves evolved into the kind of entity that we know today. They now appear as little grumpy old men who are perhaps really kind at heart. They are physically sturdy and extremely single-minded and are supposedly great warriors. However, vestiges of their fiery temper and extreme intransigence remain. They have become the prototype of the quintessential dwarf: Gimli, son of Gloin, in J.R.R. Tolkien's *Lord of the Rings.* Also remaining was their suspicion of Humankind, whom they generally regarded as weak and vacillating. It is said that they keep to themselves, continuing to inhabit deep caves and mines where they work in metal and extract ores from the rock. Others may live deep in the forests, amongst the roots of trees, but they, too, often work as smiths or metalworkers, and shun humans as much as possible. In more modern folklore, they became figures of fun and their image lightened somewhat, with more positive attributes, such as loyalty and trustworthiness. But in some cases vestiges of the older, grimmer beings often survived. They are still wary, still acerbic, and they still work with metal in forges under the earth. The notion of the dark underground entities certainly hasn't gone away.

Trolls

Indeed some of the dwarves' darker traits had been passed to another type of fairy that lived in deep caves, gullies, and ravines: the troll. Like the idea of both the dwarf and the kobold, the idea of the troll probably originated in Scandinavia. And in many respects the troll may have had its beginnings in the idea of the walking dead, because it corresponds closely to the idea of the lumbering *draugr*, the walking corpse of Norse folklore, which was known as a shambling, rather vacuous entity with immense strength. However, there is a slight problem as to what the troll actually looked like. In some tales, it is described as a towering if rather stupid monstrous creature, living high in mountain caves. They have flat, brutish faces, sometimes with long, lower tusks and perhaps a single eye in the center of their foreheads. This image perhaps comes from the Norwegian *jotnar* (giants), who were huge primitive beings living a brutish existence in the caves and caverns of the underearth. They were also known as *jaette* in both Sweden and Denmark, and the idea of these gigantic slow-witted trolls appears to have emerged from that concept. The idea has also found its way into some of the English perceptions as well, perhaps through the Viking occupation of that country, where it appears in places such as Trollers Gill and Trollerdale, near Appletreewick in Yorkshire, in an area known as the Barden Triangle. Here among the tumbled and grotesquely formed rocks, huge, violent trolls are supposed to dwell, giving the region its name. However, in some cases, the trolls are described as blood-drinking goblins—harking back, perhaps, to the old notion of dwarves and the dwarfish species as vampires. The large English species is perhaps more akin to ogres, and in many tales are often described as such.

In the southern part of Scandinavia, however, a slightly different concept regarding trolls seems to have emerged. Here, the trolls are much smaller, and, although still primitive in their ways and brutish in appearance, they more resembled the huldufolk discussed earlier. However, in stories about them they seem to be more deformed and more malignant than any of the huldufolk; so much so that it has been suggested that the word *troll* may come from an ancient southern Scandinavian word meaning "someone who behaves violently or flagrantly," and that the original trolls in this region may not have been supernatural at all, but rather some form of human outlaws. Others, however, have stated that the word is in fact Germanic and refers to some form of skill or art with supernatural and malignant connotations. They point to an early Germanic word, *trolldom*, meaning "witchcraft" or "spell working" in an antisocial sense.

In Scandinavian folklore there is also some confusion as to whether trolls live alone or in groups. In the northern areas where they are said to be giants, they tend to live alone in very deep caves, well away from human settlements. In the south they live in communities close to the surface where they can sometimes interact with Humankind. In the Faroe Islands, where they are known as "trows" (as they are in some northerly British places like Orkney), stories tend to center on the interaction between the fairy kind and humans—a relationship that is not always to the mortals' benefit. Sometimes the trow will attach itself to one particular family and, while not especially malignant, will become something of a nuisance.

In most cases these types of underground spirit—kobold, dwarf, and troll—are seldom seen, but make their presence known through the medium of sound. Individuals passing through lonely or isolated mountain valleys or working in confined spaces such as caves or mines have often heard unaccountable sounds such as voices or rappings, which they have tried to rationalize by attributing to the fairy kind. This may be the origin of the belief in "knockers"—a type of Cornish fairy related to the kobold—which was (and still is) held by Cornish tin-miners in the South of England. They were said to warn of (or sometimes cause) rockfalls within the confines of the mine, but might also perhaps steal and hide workmens' and miners' tools. They might draw miners deeper into the hills where they might become lost and maybe even die. Some might throw stones at men as they worked in underground mines and caves, very much in the manner of the Slu-agh on the surface above. Many Cornish miners complained of being struck by elfbolts, thrown by unseen beings, down in the darkness of their mines. Usually the throwing of such a missile was followed by a series of raps, which gave the fairies their name. "Knockers" were considered to be rather mischievous, but could be either malignant or downright evil if the mood took them.

Various precautions had to be taken before going down into the mines. For example, pieces of bread or small cakes had to be tak-en down into the dark to be left as offerings for the fairies. Miners should not whistle nor, for some reason, use the word *hare* while un-derground, because this was sure to encourage a rockfall or a sudden emission of dangerous gasses (two persistent fears of many miners). It is, of course, easy to dismiss these ideas as quaint superstition and make light of them, but to the Cornish miners, as William Chester-ton pointed out in his pamphlet *Cornish Traditions* (published 1834), these were serious and had to be scrupulously observed.

Goblins

Another fairy, closely allied to kobolds and trolls, and certainly considered malignant and dangerous, was the goblin. These were small (about the height of a 2-year-old child) malformed creatures, with twisted, crabby features and spiteful ways. Although in folkloric terms, the fairy seems to be confined to Britain, the source of the name is probably French—*gobelin*—which may be a form of *gobel* taken from the Germanic kobold. Goblins were described as small and malformed, and although they did not technically live deep under-ground, they often inhabited caves and burrows in the forests. Some legends appear to class them as wanderers without having any sort of permanent home, yet some others describe them as dwelling in cav-erns or under the roots of trees. Arguably, of all the fairies, the goblins had the closest associations with death because, in early French and English traditions, they were supposed to inhabit the areas beneath old funerary mounds and tumuli scattered across the countryside. Not only this, but some early representations of goblins in Britain appear to show them with skull-like faces and bony hands, suggestive of decay and of corpses. In places such as France and parts of Germany they have an ambivalent temperament—neither good nor evil—but in Britain they are regarded as especially dangerous. Like the unquiet dead they were incredibly hostile toward the living and constantly sought ways to disadvantage or harm individuals, or even Mankind in general. This they did by trickery and subterfuge, seeking by their wiles to lead decent humans astray. They were sly and, although sometimes pretending to be sympathetic toward humans, were always seeking ways to injure or kill them. In fact, in some parts of Germany the same *gobel* was sometimes used to describe a wastrel or a tricky person who lived by his or her wits (usually by dubious means and at the expense of others).

In some stories goblins were supposed to drink blood (making them akin to vampires) or eat flesh (making them cannibalistic). They were, according to many tales, monsters in a miniature form, often displaying terrible attributes—the very embodiment of the evil walking dead. The terms *goblin* and *phantom* often became interchangeable in certain areas of England (for example in Yorkshire).

And yet, in some parts of Europe, there seems to be at least some interchange between goblins and humans. In some parts of France, for example, goblins were tradesmen and used open-air markets (as did human traders) in order to sell their wares. Old tales from places such as Provence and Brittany sometimes speak of small markets controlled by goblin traders set up in isolated parts of the countryside late at night to which humans might go in order to buy items. These were usually held under oak trees or in the bushes well away from prying eyes, and only humans who knew that they were there traded with the goblins. However, the inbuilt wariness of the goblin kind still persisted in such places. If the goblins sold food, for example, it might be poisonous to humans; if they sold crockery or metalware, it might turn brittle and break shortly after purchase; money that was received from the goblins in change would turn to leaves, acorns, or manure as soon as daylight touched it. Humans had to be extremely careful when attempting to deal with the goblin people.

So malignant was the goblin that the name has become attached to almost any kind of small, evil, bad-tempered sprite. For example, the *tomtin,* the vicious characters dressed invariably in red who accompanied Santa Claus on his rounds in medieval and early-modern Germany, are often described as goblins. These are not to be confused with the Swedish *tomte,* who are often considered to be beneficial and protective house spirits. Tomtin, who travel with Santa Claus, are of a much more malignant and violent nature. Santa, of course, has not always been the kindly old soul that we know today; at one time he was as much feared as welcomed. In the depths of winter, he would travel from house to house accompanied by the goblin-like and demonic tomtin, to wake children from their sleep and make them recite their Christian catechism to prove their goodness and holiness. If they recited correctly, they received a gift, but if they made even the smallest mistake they would be brutally beaten with chains by the tomtin. This belief gave Santa Claus his German nickname of *Bullerklaus* (Bell Nicholas), because the clank of the chains carried by the goblin tomtin resembled the clang of a bell. The tomtin would later become "sanitized" and would be transformed into "Santa's little helpers," but their original incarnation was that of a sadistic and malignant spirit, intent on bringing violence to young children. In some cases they were described as vampires who drank the blood of the youngsters who had misbehaved during the course of the year. Hardly a cheery Christmas festivity!

The idea of the goblin (or a roughly similar creature) was also attached to various other winter visitors or gift bearers who came in the dark time before the end of the year either to reward or to punish their followers. One of these was Nacht Ruprecht (Night Rupert), who traveled through the harsh winters of medieval Bavaria to bestow gifts on those who had faithfully worshipped him throughout the year and to chastise those who had neglected to do so. He seems to have been some sort of nature spirit—a dark and hideous creature of straw and roots, somewhat like a scarecrow—and he was usually accompanied by a vicious goblin-creature named George Oaf. Similar to the tomtin, Oaf carried a large, studded flail, which he used mercilessly to whip those who had been negligent in their worship of the forest deities or who had accepted Christianity, lapping up any spilled blood like

a dog. It was said that the creature was also cannibalistic and would frequently bite some of its victims with a grisly relish. George Oaf was described as a goblin, but was actually thought to be the spirit of someone long dead.

It seems clear that in many folktales goblins and goblin-like beings were connected with the period around winter and the dark times of the year. This was also a time that was associated with death and decay, a time when ghosts and phantoms were at their most active. If they did live under the ground, then they inhabited former Pagan graveyards and certain pre-Christian enclosures, for they were associated with old gods as well, and acted as helpers to them.

In the Baltic states and in Finland, goblins were known as *hiisi*—named after one of the 12 sons of Keleva, king of Kainuu, who appears in the Kalevala (an epic poem based on ancient Finnish folklore compiled by Elias Lonnrot [1802–1884] from various traditional sources such as rural storytellers). These were creatures closely resembling goblins and/or trolls who inhabited various remote and rocky places around the Finnish coast. In the Estonian language, the word meant "holy place," but it could also be taken to mean any place that was wild and untamed, which was the traditional habitation for such fairies. There was no agreement on the size of hiisi—similar to trolls they could be gigantic or small dwarves—but it was generally agreed that they were extremely evil. Emerging from their burrows, they would process through the Baltic countryside on certain nights of the year—a procession that resembled the Macara Shee to which Yeats alluded in Ireland—roistering and making noise and attacking any whom they met. If people happened to leave the doors of their houses open for any reason, the hiisi would enter and steal something of value to the household, either financial or sentimental. In Finland, hiisi are used to explain geological features and ancient prehistoric structures left by former inhabitants; for example, deep stone crevices or potholes formed by swirling water are known as hiisi's cauldrons (*hiidenkimu*). In England and Ireland, they are usually known as giants' kettles.

There was little that could be done to turn away the hiisi, save perhaps for the blessing of a priest, although, like many fairies in Westernized cultures they did show a particular aversion to iron. In some instances a talisman, made entirely of iron, inscribed with a holy word, was hung on the lintel of a door in order to prevent them from entering a house, but this was perhaps the only protection that could be offered. If one was pursued by the hiisi, then the best thing to do was to run toward cultivated ground; because the fairies were creatures of the wilderness, they would probably be loath to set foot there, although this was not always the case and the protection could not be relied upon.

All these figures—kobolds, knockers, dwarves, trolls, goblins, and hiisi—all appear to have their roots in Germanic and Scandinavian lore (transferred to places such as England) and may all come from the same root source or central idea. They were probably the last remnants of the old nature spirits or a notion of the unquiet dead still seeking to make their presence known in the living world. In this they fitted into a recognizable context. Beings such as the tomtin or George Oaf, perhaps not strictly goblins but goblin-like creatures—also fit into such a context as servitors of either the old gods or the dead.

More problematic, however, are the *kallikantzaroi,* a race of Greek fairies who are believed to be actively working to bring about the end of the world. Like the kobolds and dwarves they too are artisans, although they are said to work in wood rather than in metal. Setting their legend within a Christian context, it is believed that they are ordained by God to ensure that the world ends at a certain time, and to this end they are employed in sawing through the roots of the World Tree, which is believed to hold everything together. When the roots are finally cut through and the Tree falls, the world will end and everything will pass away. A belief in these beings is an interesting fusion of both Christian and Pagan interpretation.

Kallikantzaroi

The kallikantzaroi live far underground working away at the roots of the Tree almost in total darkness. However, in the colder months, they tend to gravitate toward the surface, appearing there at night (their eyes being unused to sunlight) in order to do harm or mischief to humans. This was the only time they set aside their work, and they take a perverse pleasure in the damage they do within the living world.

As soon as Christmas passes, they return underground to continue their sawing (usually around Epiphany, which is January 6). In the interim, the World Tree has healed itself and so they start from the beginning again.

There is no real origin given for the kallikantzaroi or a reason as to why they should seek the destruction of the entire world (other than the Christian assertion that they have been instructed to do so by God). Not even their name provides a clue, as it is usually taken to mean "beautiful centaur" (although they appear to have no obvious connections with the half-men, half-horse beings of ancient Thessaly, and they are often said to be deformed and hideous to look at). However, it is said that anyone born between the 17th and 26th of December (the old Roman Saturnalia—a festival of unbridled licentiousness) is in grave danger of becoming one of their number. This may be no more than a reaction of the Orthodox Church to the ancient Pagan feast times and against those who still observed them. In fact, anyone born during this time may run the risk of becoming one of the kallikantzaroi for a brief time during the Christmas period starting in adulthood, and permanently becoming one after death. The only protection is to wrap the newborn baby in straw and garlic and to singe its toenails with a red-hot iron—somewhat extreme for an infant!

There are no standard descriptions of the kallikantzaroi, except that they are invariably male and have exceeding large genitalia. In some tales concerning them, they are depicted as being naked, in other stories they are dressed in heavy clothing, "like a peasant." Their faces are said to be intensely ugly and malevolent, but that is where any similarity ends. A number of tales cannot even agree about their size—some describe them as about the size of an average human being, others as being very small.

An effective method to stop them from entering a house is to place a colander or scatter peas around the doorstep. Similar to vampires, the kallikantzaroi are particularly obsessive creatures and they will stop to count the number of holes or peas have been scattered in the colander. Because none of them can count above three (three being a holy number), this is likely to take some time—at least until the sun comes up and, fearing the daylight, they are forced to return to the underground. If they cannot enter through the door, however, it was assumed that they will come down the chimney in order to gain entrance (their extremely large genitalia permitting), and so it is considered advisable to have a fire burning all night in the fireplace in order to prevent this.

Karakoncolos

The kallikantzaroi fairies also have a parallel in Anatolian Turkey and in Bulgaria where they are known as *karakoncolos.* These beings are roughly the same as in Greece, but are covered with a kind of reddish hair or fur; they were widely regarded as bogeymen in the days of the Ottoman Empire. They appear during the first 10 days of Zemheri—the period of "dreadful cold" (winter)—and attempt to lure people from their houses by calling them out, imitating the voices of their friends. It is further believed that they can alter their shape to their victim, and if the charm is not broken, the unfortunate will freeze to death in the dead of winter. Some depictions of them show them standing on a rise with a sharp-bladed harrow, which they wield like a weapon. They will halt travelers on the road and ask them ordinary questions, which, even if the answer is correct, they will use as an excuse to cut their victims to shreds with the harrow. To avoid this, the answer must include the Turkish word *kara* meaning "black," which will somehow frustrate the karakoncolos's intent, and they must return to their underground burrows once more.

Duende

Many of the characteristics that define the kallikantzaroi also apply to another species of fairy in a different part of the world. These are the duende, a type of fairy to be found in Spain, Portugal, and parts of Hispanic South America. In Spain, they are supposed to live under the ground among the foundations of certain houses, and the name itself comes from the Spanish word *duendo* meaning "the real owner of the house." It is possible that originally they were some form of protective home spirit like a hobgoblin (initially a spirit associated with the hearth), and later the word became applied in a much wider sense. Duendes would appear to be characterized by their headgear—they wear enormously large hats that throw their wizened, goblin-like faces into shadow and give them a distinctly sinister appearance. As soon as night fell and the inhabitants of the house were asleep, they emerged from under the floorboards and began all sorts of mischief such as breaking plates, overturning piles of food, and turning milk bad. In parts of Portugal it is believed that the duende can also bring disease into a house so that individuals will wake up ill after going to bed feeling well. In the Spanish mountains, it is believed that the duende will emerge from under houses in order to clip the toenails of very young children (particularly those who haven't been washed before being put to bed) with great scissors or blades, causing them immense pain and perhaps even cutting of their toes. In order to prevent this, the feet off all infants must be rubbed with garlic, which will allegedly drive the creatures away, because it is thought that they find the smell of garlic remarkably offensive.

Gradually the fairies generally moved out of the houses and into the wider woodlands where they continued to live underground in burrows like small animals. But there they continue their mischief and evil ways. For example, they try to lead travelers (particularly young girls) astray deep in the forest, so that they cannot find their way home by imitating human voices calling to them. When they are completely lost and exhausted, the duende leap upon them and seek to impregnate them with their immensely large phalluses. Thus, a number of illegitimate children in both Spain and Portugal may be duende offspring. The way to tell is to look at their thumbs, which will be slightly misshapen. Thumbs are a total giveaway as far as these fairies are concerned. In Brazil, Belize, and parts of Honduras, there is a widespread belief that the forest duende (or *Tata duende* as they are sometimes known) are roughly the same height as any human being, and it is also believed that they can easily be detected because they have no thumbs on either hand. Their fingernails, however, are remarkably long and hooked, and these are used for digging or extending their burrows in the forest.

Although there are no strong associations with the dead concerning kallikantzaroi or duende, there may be hints in some legends of connection to some forgotten races. In some areas—for example, Belize—the Tata duende are sometimes known as "the old ones" or "the other ones," suggesting, perhaps, a race of people that may have retreated underground or deep into the forests at some point. Curiously, the same phrase is often used to describe fairies in Celtic countries where, as we have seen, they were sometimes regarded as a race that was separate from Mankind—in many parts of Ireland, for instance, they are frequently referred to as "the other crowd," and this is not always said in a complimentary fashion. However, in some folklore, fairies (particularly malignant ones living underground) form a kind of "half-way house" between ancient races and the dead.

It is worth noting in passing that in Spain the capriciousness and unpredictability of the duende have found their way into popular and artistic culture. The term, which is hard to define, denotes a certain passion or improvisation among artists and dancers (particularly among those who dance the flamenco) that gives the work or performance its depth. Although it may be exaggerating to say that the fairy is somehow connected to the idea of the muse, certain parallels are evident. Nevertheless, the notion of duende as fairies still maintains its central connections with peoples who have gone before and with spirits and ghosts.

Taotaomonas

This certainly appears to be the case amongst the Chomorro peoples of the Northern Mariana Islands of Micronesia (which includes Guam), who have been subject to Spanish influence for many centuries. Here there is a belief in taotaomonas, a sort of fairy-like being that is not unrelated to the duende, and is halfway between the remnants of an ancestral race and the spirits of the dead. The Guahan people, who were the original inhabitants of these islands, are said to have lived in the islands between 1485 and 500 BC, but there may have been earlier peoples dwelling there before them. Similar to trolls, the taotaomonas appear to fall into two categories: big and menacing or small and stealthy. The latter is said to have originated after Spanish missionaries reached the islands—they discouraged worship of the ancestors and, bereft of such devotions, the taotaomonas gradually shrank in size over a period of time. In some legends they are described as being without heads, with their still-active torsos being both twisted and deformed. But no account can really agree on what they look like. Only two things about them are certain: they lived under the ground, as perhaps did the early peoples, and they only emerged into the upper world around twilight. They are described as "ancestral men" (old ones), spirits, or fairies (although in this case, the two terms are interchangeable), who live in the jungle in burrows or in caves along the seashore. The taotaomonas despise anyone who is weak, so if one suspects that one is close it is necessary to talk loudly and boastfully about one's prowess in the hope that it will treat you with respect. Similarly, when gathering herbs near the mouth of a cave it is necessary to ask permission from the taotaomonas before commencing the task. It may even be necessary to make some offering in order to show respect, or else some misfortune will surely follow.

Taotaomona society seems to be organized a tribal basis, perhaps as the early societies of the Marianas were. However, their supreme leader appears to be known as Anufat, a gigantic creature, incredibly ugly, with teeth and tusks more than 6 inches long and with holes in each side of his head, symbolizing battle wounds, from which bunches of ferns and greenery appear to be growing. He also has hands like shovels with great hooked nails resembling fish-hooks. He is said to live underground in an old cemetery somewhere among the islands, although the exact location seems to shift with each story, and each locality claims some connection with him. When passing through any cemetery it is advisable to whistle to advise Anufat of one's presence, because if he suddenly becomes aware of it, he will become alarmed and may rise and cause great harm and destruction. However, any taotaomona can be just as dangerous. They will invisibly pinch travelers with their long fingernails as they pass by their dwelling places (mounds and caves), leaving painful bruises and red welts, which will not heal, and the victim may become extremely ill. The only effective remedy for these is to visit a *suruhanu* (a male witch-doctor or healer) or a *suruhana* (female witch-doctor) in order to obtain medicines to alleviate the suffering. Certain suruhanus also claim to possess spells and incantations that will drive the taotaomonas away to protect travelers, but such protections are often suspect. Although the taotaomona usually go about invisibly, it is still possible to see them by taking the sleep residue from the eye of a dog and rubbing it into one's own eye. The taotaomonas can then been seen quite clearly, although the vision of their horrible physical appearance may be enough to strike the viewer blind.

The idea of the taotaomona, lying as it does somewhere between remnants of a lost race and ghostly ancestral spirits (the descriptions "fairy" and "ghost" can apply to these creatures in equal measure) may have something to do with the colonization and Christianization of the islands by the Spanish. There seems little doubt that before the coming of Spanish priests, the indigenous Chomorro peoples did maintain some sort of fragmented religion that involved ancestor worship. With the establishment of the Christian Church, such worship was driven underground and reemerged in the idea of spirits living underground or in the forests. Just as in Ireland and other parts of the Celtic world, this was probably blended with the race memories of some form of aboriginal race that may have lived there before the Chomorro came to form something slightly more substantial and cohesive than mere ghosts—that is, fairies.

Eastern Fairy Origins

Throughout the years these beings have become magnified by a succession of storytellers and have been gradually woven into the fabric of local legend and myth. This is perhaps the way in which most fairy stories—and indeed the fairy beliefs—have grown up within communities and have become part of accepted tradition.

The word *fairy* has therefore often become interchangeable with the name of any form of spirit, ancestral being, or race, and has become an umbrella term for many of them without ever being all that specific.

In Japan, for example, the word *yokai* (which can mean a fairy, a demon, a ghost, or a sprite) is used to denote beings that have perhaps come from the underworld to do harm to the living. Some of these beings have characteristics that are both human and animal,

some have distorted human facial elements, and all are supernatural and wholly malignant.

Kappas

One of the most common and dangerous forms of the *yokai* are the *kappa*, or river children who lived in burrows, holes, or hollows along riverbanks. They are described as being largely humanoid, about the height of a small child, but completely covered with hair or fur (these are known as *hyosube*), or even a weed-like substance. Their faces are wizened like those of monkeys, sometimes with great fang-like teeth, and some depictions of them show beaks or duck-like bills. Some other representations show them covered in scales like giant frogs, and they emit an odor like rotting fish. The kappas' most notable characteristic is the shallow, water-filled depression in the center of its crown from which weeds and ferns grow. This is, in fact, the very essence of the entity—the area from which it is said to draw its incredible strength—and if that water is spilled the yokai will simply disappear forever or else will be immobilized and turned to stone.

The kappa are considered highly dangerous, although like most fairies (and beings of a similar nature) their behavior varies according to their mood. At best they resort to mischievous pranks, such as loudly passing wind at formal gatherings, playfully lifting women's kimonos to expose their bottoms, or stealing clothing and personal items. At worst they can steal away small children, which they then drown in the river and eat. Indeed, they have a special predilection for the flesh of young children, although they may eat adults as well. However, it can be diverted by drawing it away with a large cucumber—the only form of food the *kappa* enjoys more than the flesh of young children (in fact there is a form of sushi cucumber roll named after it—the kappamaki).

Kappa are incredibly intelligent and can both understand and speak Japanese, as well as several other languages. They can hold long and philosophical discussions, and can sometimes solve puzzles that perplex the human brain. Their intelligence makes them particularly tricky, because they are continually contriving ways and means of leading humans astray and of seizing their young children. They can engage local people in pleasant conversation whilst assessing how to best them and steal from them. However, should an individual realize what is going on, the kappa will attack him or her using its phenomenal strength.

The only tried and trusted way to defeat the kappa, according to most folklorists and commentators, is really to draw the water from the depression in its head, which takes away its strength and being. To do this is a relatively simple task. Kappas are incredibly formal and polite beings with a high sense of etiquette, and so if one bows to it, the kappa will invariably consider it good manners to bow in response. As it does so, the water in the depression will spill out and be lost. Its strength will ebb away and it will be open to attack. It might even turn to stone or dust and blow away in the breeze. However, a word of warning: In some stories, the loss of the water simply allows the kappa to live on land, where it can create more evil, and this will infuriate it, so that it will become even more malicious. Its strength may very well increase, as may its violence. Kappa are always very difficult to deal with.

The origins of this fairy creature (if we may use that term) are very difficult to discern. Perhaps, like many of the fairies of Westernized culture, they are the embodiment of old nature spirits. Indeed, in the Shrine Shinto religion, they are taken to be some form of minor deity (*suijin*) and are sometimes described as "the souls of the water." Here, the line between what we might term as "fairies" and ancient deities (and even demons) becomes rather blurred, and, as we have seen, the terms are often interchangeable.

Huli Jing

This is also certainly the case with the Chinese *huli jing,* which are perhaps the closest ideal to Westernized spirits that we can find in the Far East. These beings—also known as fox spirits—often dwell in caverns among the roots of trees and only come out at night, thus resembling the animal after which they are named. In Chinese folklore it is believed that animals can often take the form of humans and acquire some supernatural powers while still retaining some of their animalistic characteristics, such as, say, living in burrows. The huli jing, however, seem slightly more human than they do fox. But they are immortal, provided they can obtain sufficient energy from ordinary humans to sustain themselves. To do this, they lure mortals away by pretending to be either beautiful women or handsome young men (this is, in fact, an illusion, because in reality they have the sharp features of foxes), and when alone, surreptitiously drawing of their energy by a process akin to osmosis (usually, though not necessarily, carried out through a sexual act). In this respect they are little more than vampires. If they cannot acquire sufficient energy, they will gradually lose height and dwindle away like a candle flame until there is nothing left of them.

Descriptions of the huli jing vary. In some legends they are the same size as ordinary Chinese people, and in others they are slightly smaller. Their faces are sharp and feral-looking, and they also have a tail that displays their fox origins. Their teeth are very sharp and their hands may sometimes resemble claws even when they are in human guise. They are also great illusionists and can take the form either of friends known to their victims, or of the dead. By assuming the appearance of known people, the huli jing can then infiltrate groups of people for their own sinister purposes.

The main way to detect a huli jing when in human form, according to tradition, is to get it drunk, when it will automatically revert to its true shape. Once this is done, it is imperative to seek out its fox's tail and to cut it off, because without the tail the being will be powerless and will shrivel up. If someone suspects a huli jing in an assembly, then there is another method of detection. A paper shape of a fox might be produced (this is known as a *spirit paper*) and secretly burned. As soon as the paper is consumed, any huli jing within the immediate vicinity will be forced to resume its original shape and can be captured.

One of the main evils that the huli jing are reputed to spread all across Southeast Asia is known as *koro*, and for obvious reasons is greatly feared. This is another name for a recognized medical condition known as GRS—Genital Retraction Syndrome—in which the male genitals and the female breasts appear to retract into the body almost to the point of disappearance. This has been diagnosed as being part of a psychosomatic hysterical complex (the condition, which appears in some parts of Africa as well, may be culture-specific). It has even, in some cases, been put down to mass hysteria, but in many rural communities this is ascribed to the activities of the huli jing, as they seek to disrupt human society. In other Chinese societies, these beings are closely associated with the spread of plague and disease, bringing illnesses from deep in the wild forests to spread amongst civilized centers.

So what are the origins of the huli jing, and can they really be counted as "fairies"? Certainly they seem to emerge from the same source as our Westernized sprites—as perhaps a form of ancient god or nature spirit and may even resemble them in some ways. If we are to use the word *goblin* in its widest possible context then it would probably be true to label them as such. And they are certainly classed as being malignant as any such sprite, sharing many of their tricky characteristics. And also like many of these Western fairies, they have to be shown respect. Those passing along certain trails in the woods or forests must first ask permission of the huli jing, as do those collecting water from wells and streams. Not to do so is to invite serious misfortune. Many of these practices are similar to those surrounding Westernized ideas of malignant and capricious fairies, so although they retrain many characteristics of Far Eastern culture, the huli jing can fit into this category as well.

Nunnehi

It would be remiss when considering such fairy creatures not to examine the concept of the nunnehi, a form of being that exists in Cherokee Indian legend, because these dwell underground and have already been alluded to earlier. According to Cherokee legend, the nunnehi were small humanoid beings who dwelt in underground caverns chiefly under the round hills that characterize part of North Carolina, and who came to the surface only once in a while. Similar to many of the fairy-kind, their motives for doing so were often ambiguous. In some tales, they are simply curious to see what the upper world is like, but in many they come from the underground to cause mischief or to injure those who live there. Tales of both monstrous creatures and strange races emerging from some underground realm are, as we have seen, abundant in Cherokee folklore. The legend of Judaculla, the giant chieftain who appeared in Jackson County to carve symbols on a rock, has already been referred to, and in the same area (the Nantahala Gorge—between Wesson and Nantahala, North Carolina) there is also the legend of Ugulu, the gigantic insect who came to the surface world "with certain of his tribe" (other giant insects) to create havoc amongst the Cherokee villages. The idea of a small race of men living under the hills is not unusual. In fact, some old Cherokee stories tell of the nunnehi coming to the surface in order to trade goods with the early human tribes—they were credited with first bringing metal artifacts to the surface from their own world. However, they were very tricky and used these trading expeditions to steal valuable items that they then took back underground. In some cases they even managed to steal livestock while the Cherokee were away on hunting expeditions.

The name *nunnehi* has a confusing origin. It is said to be a very old Cherokee word meaning "people who can live anywhere," although some linguists dispute this and say that the name means "people who live forever" (the nunnehi were believed to be immortal). Where they actually came from is unclear, because they were not considered to be another race of men, but spirit beings instead. There is no real origin given for them, but they seem to have emerged from dreams or from the thoughts of the primal gods who once ruled the earth. Finding the land already populated, the gods retreated into the underearth, but harbored a resentment against those who lived on the surface and enjoyed the sunlight while they had to put up with darkness. Therefore, they tried to drive our ancestors from the upper earth so that they could take their place. This is given as the reason why they are so hostile and malicious toward humans.

In some cases, however, they can be quite approachable and friendly, and there are some old stories about how the nunnehi guided Cherokee children who had become lost in the forest and aided hunters in finding food, or helped woodsmen in their work. Although they may have supernatural powers (for instance, they are immortal), these are not stressed to any great extent, and so the nunnehi simply become another race that lived apart from the mainstream.

Gradually, as time went on, the nunnehi seem to have become more and more reclusive. One of the supernatural powers they *do* appear to have is invisibility, and this they seem to have used every time they visited the surface world. They also seem to have decreased in height, thus becoming more difficult to spot, even when they were not invisible. If they *were* seen it was only for the briefest of moments, and contact with humans tended to be minimal. However, they sometimes left evidence of their passing in the form of curiously shaped stones, sometimes known as "fairy crosses." These are small pieces of stone-like or calcified material (thought by some to be a form of slate), which seem to have been hammered into the form of a cross and dropped along the side of mountain trails for human travelers to find. They are considered to be lucky or unlucky depending on who finds them—they have nothing to do with the recognized Christian symbol (the Cross, of course, is a much older symbol than Christianity). There are a number of local tales concerning these fairy crosses—some saying that they were made from rare and precious gemstone, polished to perfection, and that whoever found one of them would be wealthy. Other legends stated that they were the crystallized tears of the nunnehi women, and if found they would bring only pain and misfortune to the finder.

Although the nunnehi are closely associated with Cherokee lands (their name itself is thought to be derived from ancient Cherokee), they appear in a number of areas of America, even as far south as New Mexico. Their main geographical area is, however, North Carolina and Tennessee, particularly deep into the mountain reaches of the Appalachians. Their activities seem to be centered on an area that is known as "the balds" or the "bald hills." These are round hills or low mountains on the summits of which nothing grows. A number of them are believed to be hollow—"the hollow hills"—somehow resulting in this curious geographical phenomenon. Strange lights and noises have often been seen and heard around these hills, and this has given them a somewhat mysterious and supernatural reputation. Sounds such as distant drumming have often drifted down from the summits of the balds, and this has been attributed to the drumming of the unseen nunnehi—the little people under the hills. The lights seen on the slopes of the "balds" were the fires that the nunnehi had lit to signal their festivities as they came to the surface world. Anyone who chanced on these dances without an invite would never leave again.

It is claimed in some lore that these "balds" stand on top of an immense underground network of caverns in which the nunnehi dwell. At the very center of this system a great flame burns, rising up from the core of the world. This, say the legends, is the very essence of our world, and the nunnehi have been placed there to guard and maintain it. In other versions of the tale, it is a well of "spiritual water" that lies down there, but the function of the nunnehi remains the same.

Although these "little people" originated in Cherokee legend, the white settlers who came to the area were mainly of Irish and Scots stock—a people who had their own stories of "little men" in their own countries. It was easy to transpose tales of the nunnehi onto the incoming Scots-Irish tradition and give them an even stronger emphasis. The original Indian entities became equated, therefore, with leprechauns and brownies, although they still retained some elements of Cherokee belief—such as drumming somewhere among the hills and lighting distant fires. They were still believed to reside underground in some dark and gloomy kingdom, only coming to the surface once in a while and usually under the cover of darkness. And they still retained at least some of their hostility toward Mankind in general, as well as their "tricky" or "malicious" nature. In many ways, too, they were much more dangerous than the leprechauns and pixies of Irish and Scottish legend, because they went out of their way to drive away livestock (on which the settlers depended for their survival in wild and remote places), and also kidnapped small children and took them back to their underground realm.

In later stories, the idea of the nunnehi seems to have undergone a slight change. They became shapeshifters, able to take on the guise of any bird or animal, and their magical powers appear to have increased. They also became kinder and gentler toward humans, as the stories of them helping lost hunters and travelers increased. Perhaps the idea of them has been influenced by some Westernized concepts of European fairies, which had been brought into certain areas by the white settlers; perhaps Indian lore concerning them was also undergoing a change in its emphasis. The nunnehi also seemed to have a greater liking for Westernized music (even in Cherokee tradition, the nunnehi were supposed to be skilled and talented musicians), and would sometimes come from their world of invisibility to peer in at cabin windows where a dance or party was in progress. Indeed, as time went on, these beings were now rapidly approaching an ideal of what we in the West would consider fairies to be like, and perhaps this was essentially due to a fusion of Indian lore with settler myth.

As well as being associated with the "balds," the nunnehi are connected with an Indian mound near the town of Franklin, North Carolina. The town overlooks the valley of the Little Tennessee River and was built on the site of an ancient Cherokee sacred council place where important meetings were held. All around was the sacred Cherokee city of Nikwasi, which seems to have been centered on the mound. In fact, the Mound seems to be a way into the nunnehi world through which they come and go to and from ours. Through this Mound (and similar structures) they can also view the upper world and sometimes express their disapproval at the actions of its inhabitants.

In the years 1811 and 1812 a series of severe earthquakes struck the region around New Madrid in the Missouri Bootheel, causing loss of life and alarming the Creek Indians who were living there. This was said to be from the activities of the nunnehi and was taken to mean that they were angry at the closeness and cooperation between Indians and white men, of which they disapproved. This led to the formation of the Red Stick Movement among Indian groups (chiefly the Creeks), that said Indian nations would return to their tradition-al ways, and ultimately to the Red Stick War of 1813–14 in which the emerging United States became embroiled. It is further said that the prominent Red Stick leader William Weatherford (Red Eagle) was guided and advised by the nunnehi. Whether this is true or not, it would seem that the little people are not averse to becoming involved in American politics!

Moon-Eyed People

Nor are the nunnehi the only type of "fairy" living amongst the American mountains. Other legends also speak of the "moon-eyed" people—a diminutive race living in the Tennessee Mountains and along the Cumberland Plateau. Their height is given as being no high-erthan the knee of a full-grown Indian, they have pale skin and heavy beards, and are said to live deep underground along the mountain trails. According to old stories, these are a race of people who lived in the region long before the coming of the Spanish and are guardians of vast seams of gold below the surface of the earth. As such, they have (according to some accounts) formidable supernatural powers. Further, they were supposed to live in "round houses" (perhaps small circular caves) just below the surface of the earth.

As their name might suggest, the "moon-eyed people" had rather large, circular eyes that were not used to strong sunlight. In fact, they only emerged at night; if they emerged in daylight, they would most probably be blinded. In fact, so sensitive were their eyes that even during a full moon they might be blinded as well. Both the Cherokee and Creek Indians knew of their existence because of small mounds of fortifications that these people had built to protect themselves from enemies and to shield themselves from the sun.

The moon-eyes, however, had other forms of defense. They had a prodigious knowledge of herbs and potions and were skilled poison-ers. When Indian villages encroached on their lands, they systematically poisoned the nearby wells, inducing sickness and disease amongst the tribes. Nevertheless, Cherokee legend claims that the enemies of the Cherokee—the Creeks (with whom they fought a number of conflicts) had managed to overwhelm the moon-eyes in the years before recorded history, by attacking them on a moonlit night. Defeated in battle by the Creeks, the moon-eyes were driven further underground where they remain to this day, their sense of animosity, and resentment toward humans still simmering.

Yunwi Tsusdi

Both the nunnehi and the moon-eyed people are sometimes confused with Yunwi Tsusdi, another diminutive race living in the Great Smokies and with whom they appear to share many basic characteristics. It is said that the Yunwi Tsusdi are generally friendly (or at worse indifferent) toward humans except when one attempts to find out where they live or the location of their towns (these are said to be either deep in the forest or far underground and accessed by caves). Cherokee and Creek lore are full of stories concerning people who have died after following the Yunwi Tsusdi to their secret dwelling places. Similar to the moon-eyes, the Yunwi Tsusdi are skilled in herbal lore and can concoct various poisonous potions that they use to kill humans. And like all the little people of the mountains they have the power of invisibility, which means they can only be seen occasionally. In this respect they appear to be very like European fairies.

Whether it be kobolds, goblins, trolls, or nunnehi, the underground (and the deep, dark forest glades) seems to be teeming with diminutive fairy-like creatures, many of whom have an innate antipathy toward Mankind. They may even use their considerable powers to take humans away from the world of light to their dark underground realm to live as servants and slaves. Fairy abduction, of course, is not a novel concept in folklore—fairies have allegedly been "taking individuals away" in one form or another for centuries, and it is to this aspect of fairy lore and belief that we now turn.

Chapter 4

Away With
the Fairies

I n a remote area of County Sligo during the late 1800s a little boy and girl were playing quite happily near the crossroads close to their cottage. It was late in the afternoon and the light was starting to fade, casting long shadows down the road and across the surrounding countryside. The air had grown very cold and it was almost time for the children to go inside. Suddenly, from the road that led in the direction of the distant mountains, the boy spotted a grand coach, drawn by several fine-looking horses, and he caught his sister's arm and pointed. The coach drew closer, traveling at incredible speed until it drew up just beyond the crossroads. The children stared in wonder as its door opened and a fine lady and gentleman, both grandly dressed, looked out.

"Come here children," the man called, beckoning. "I may have something for you both." The two of them advanced a little way, with the boy in the front, but it was his sister—a small, pretty girl—that the lady in the coach had fixed her eyes on, and her gaze was hard and cold.

"What a beautiful child," she murmured. The boy took another step forward.

"Is you a lord and a lady sir? One of the grand gentry?" he enquired. The man gave a high and brittle laugh, which was like a bird cry in the fields.

"We are indeed gentry after a fashion," he replied. "I am a lord in yon hills beyond—a little way from here—and this is my lady. But I promised you a gift. Show them, my dear." Reaching into the shadows of the coach, the woman brought out a large golden ball, which she held out invitingly toward the children. Their eyes widened.

"Do you like it?" the woman asked the girl, who nodded eagerly. "In our halls there are many such wonders. Perhaps you and your brother would like to see them?" She spoke slowly and enticingly. The boy, however, was on his guard. He was older than his sister and much more wary. There was something strange about this grand couple and he thought that they might not be all they said they were. But the golden ball did look inviting. All the same he hung back, but his sister showed no such hesitation. She moved forward to the coach.

"So you would like to see these wonders!" exclaimed the man. "Then you shall. You will come with us to our hall where you shall see things which you won't believe. Come up with us now and we can be there in an instant!" But the boy still hung back. "Then your sister will come with us. But I promised you a present. Would you like this wonderful golden ball?" He turned to the girl. "Do not fear my dear— there are plenty of wonderful things within our halls. You will have a marvelous time—that I can guarantee." He handed the ball to the boy and the lady held out a gloved hand to receive the girl into the coach, helping her up over the step. "Give this to your parents as a gift from me," said the grand man, handing the ball to the boy, "and tell them that their daughter will be home presently." The boy took the ball and looked at it, and suddenly the coach was gone, dashing away at breathtaking speed along the road in the direction of the far hills, carrying his sister inside. He looked down at the wonderful golden orb and all that he held in his hand was a withered and wizened turnip. Then he knew that this was fairy glamor and that his sister had been taken.

The girl's parents were, of course, distraught. Along with many of their neighbors, they wandered the roads looking for her, but found no trace. Some of her relatives even traveled as far as the fairy hills exploring the ancient forts and raths, but once again they found nothing. The little girl was gone forever, tempted away by the fairies. Whether or not she was actually experiencing the promised wonders is another question.

The idea that fairies would steal human children, as in the previous folktale, was incredibly widespread in many parts of the Celtic world. Children were vulnerable and open to temptation—factors that the fairies played upon. And once taken it was doubtful that they would be seen again in the human world. It was therefore believed in Celtic tradition (especially in Ireland and Scotland) that the fairies were constantly trying to lure human infants away from their relatives and into their own mystic realm. Indeed, this idea forms the basis of the Irish writer W.B. Yeats's celebrated poem *The Stolen Child:*

Dark Fairies

Come away O human child,
To the waters and the wild,
With a faery hand in hand,
For the world's more full of weeping than you can understand.

Although there are hints of an idyllic life, the underlying premise of abduction with all its pain, misery, and sense of loss is still there. And, of course, the stealing of vulnerable children was a real threat.

But why did the fairies actually want human children? Were they to act as slaves or servants to the fairy kind? That was one thought, and we shall return to it later, but there was another: the fairies needed human beings on which to breed for the survival of their own species, and the kidnapped children, when grown up, would eventually produce such offspring.

The Creation of Fairies

It was generally believed within the Celtic world that the act of birth among the fairies was a difficult business. There are many stories of "handy women" (local midwives) who were summoned from their houses by fairy men to come and attend their wives who were in labor. The process of birth for them was extremely long and difficult. For example, from Donegal in the very North of Ireland comes a tale of a local midwife who was summoned from her bed by a strange houseman and taken to a house somewhere near Mallin to attend to a fairy woman who was giving birth and having an extremely difficult time. Entering the house, she saw that the servants were actually the forms (ghosts?) of her dead neighbors, and one warned her not to eat or drink anything while in the place. She was offered food and drink several times, but refused on each occasion. The fairy woman gave birth—to something that was small and crooked—but it was whisked away before the woman could actually see it. On being taken home again, she was given a great gold ring as payment for her services, which turned to a circle of blood as soon as she put it in a drawer. What became of the fairy child she had no idea. A number of similar stories come from places such as Carmarthenshire in Wales, where the midwife attends a lady of the Tylwyth Teg, and from near Castletown on the Isle of Man.

Humans gave birth much more easily than the fairy kind and could carry babies for a slightly longer period (fairies were said, in some old stories, to carry their young for no longer than seven or eight months), allowing them to develop more fully. Therefore humans were best suited to carry fairy children, but only if they were taken young and "raised up" in the fairy way. In order to do this, they had to abduct small children when they were impressionable and could be easily manipulated into fairy customs and fairy thinking. This was why babies and children were so particularly at risk.

Because they were so vulnerable, newborn children were in special need of protection. It was essential to get an infant baptized as soon as possible after birth, because the blessing of a priest in baptismal water was considered in some quarters to ward off the fairy kind. Opinion, however, could be divided. Some believed that fairy magic was so strong that not even the power of a local cleric could overcome it—protection would have to come through the blessing of a high churchman, such as a bishop or cardinal, although holy water and certain relics *might* turn the fairy kind. Baptism and acceptance into the local congregation was probably the best method of safeguarding the young, as it implied the direct intervention of God himself. However, all fairies did fear iron, so perhaps this was a better form of protection than the blessings of the Church. Therefore, iron fire tongs were placed across the crib until the infant could be baptized (in many cases the custom continued as an additional safeguard until the infant was fully grown). Similarly, a coat or an item of clothing belonging to the child's father or grandfather thrown across the foot of the bed reminded the fairies that this was a human child not to be touched by them. When I was a child, my grandfather threw his shirt across the end of my bed every night specifically for this purpose (I was neither baptized nor christened, so I was particularly at risk). Once the child was abducted it was unlikely that its family would ever see it again, as it was now fairy property.

Changelings

The idea of abduction is strongly connected to the notion of fairy changelings. Sometimes the fairies did not simply leave an empty crib behind, but placed one of their own—usually an old, wizened, and crabby being—in place of the stolen child. In some cases the abduction was not even detected by the human parents for several days. They simply assumed that their child was ill or "off color" (although there were said to be some tell-tale signs such as the rapid growing of hair or teeth). However, as the days went on, the nature of the changeling became apparent. It was irritable and cried continuously; it appeared wizened and didn't thrive; it either didn't eat all that much or, like a cuckoo in the nest, it consumed vast quantities of food, placing a drain on the resources of the household, maybe to the detriment of other family members. In the end it would often die before it was very old.

Of course, the notion of the changeling usually explained the onset of infantile diseases. A mother might go to bed with a healthy child in the cradle beside her and awake to find it shrivelled and sickly. The reason was medical rather than supernatural. Infant illness coupled with epidemics of diseases such as tuberculosis often struck the young. Poor diet often played a part in this too. For example, even around the latter half of the 19th century when medical treatments were starting to slowly improve, one child in five still usually died. In places like rural Ireland, such a statistic was even higher, and many babies suffered a long and debilitating illness before eventually succumbing. They may have lost weight and become irritable in the absence of medical opinion—many remote areas remained unvisited by doctors—so their condition was often put down to fairy intervention. The explanation was that they were a changeling—a fairy put there in place of the healthy child who had been spirited away. It was difficult to tell, so in some parts of the countryside certain "tests" were devised to determine whether or not the sickly child was indeed a fairy. Some of these were rather terrible, but, argued popular wisdom, once a changeling came into the house there would be no luck there afterward; it would draw all the good out of the household. One rather barbaric method involved placing the baby on the blade of an iron shovel and holding it over an open fire. The heat and smoke from the blaze would drive the fairy (if indeed it was a fairy) away and restore the original child. Another method was to force a tea made from

foxgloves (lusmore, which was poisonous) into the child in order "to burn the entrails out of the fairy thing," and usually killing the child in the process. A less savage means of detection was to try to get the creature in the cradle to reveal its true age, because the fairy would be much older than that of the infant (possibly many hundreds of years). This method of dealing with the changeling is demonstrated in an old story, once popular in many parts of Ireland, widely known as *The Brewery of Eggshells*:

In the West of Ireland, one time, there was a poor couple living. They hadn't much, but God granted them a young son, which was their pride and joy and worth more to them than money itself. He was a healthy child and despite their poverty, they were able to keep him well fed—indeed they would have gone without themselves just to make sure he had something.

One day the man of the house went looking for work. He had been gone about a day or so when the child in the crib began to change. At first this change was very slow and the mother never noticed it. The child cried a lot and seemed to eat more than was good for it. It also looked a bit pinched but she put this down to an illness—all young babies were sick at some time. But the situation got slowly worse and by the time the father arrived back home, having found a bit of a job, the mother was seriously worried. The baby never stopped crying and though it ate vast quantities of food, it never seemed to put on any weight. It was always thin and wizened with a face on it like an old man. The woman began to worry that it might be a fairy changeling and that her own healthy baby had been taken. But how could she be sure? She went to a local wise-woman who knew about such matters and asked her. The old woman considered.

"There is only one sure way to find out," she said at last. "You must get it to reveal its true age. If it is indeed a change-ling then it will be very old and it must tell you how many years that it has lived."

"But it's a child!" exclaimed the woman in wonder. "It can't talk and tell me this!"

"These things can speak if they've a mind to," the wise woman replied. "And they can sometimes be easily tricked. Here's what you should do..." and she began to set forth a plan.

When the woman returned home, her husband was at work and the child seemed to be sleeping in its crib near the fire. Going to the pantry, the woman gathered up all the eggshells she could find and then put on a massive iron pot full of water over the fire in order to boil it up. When it was boiling she began to drop the eggshells into the bubbling water one by one. As she did so, she became aware of the eyes of the infant on her and it seemed no longer to be asleep but was watching her intently, pulling itself forward in the crib. She paid it no heed but continued to drop the eggshells into the boiling water. The child leaned even further forward in the crib, curious to see what was going on.

"What are you doing, Mammy?" it asked in a voice that seemed like that of an old, old man, creaky but full of cunning. Now the woman knew that it was a changeling that watched her, for her own child couldn't speak—and certainly not in that terrible voice. The hair stood on her neck but she kept calm, just as the wise woman had instructed.

"I am brewing, a-vic (my child)," replied the woman. The fairy creature leaned even further forward in its curiosity, gripping the sides of the crib with long and spidery fingers.

"And what are you brewing, Mammy?" it enquired.

"I am brewing eggshells a-vic." The changeling gave a high, brittle laugh and clapped its thin hands in glee.

"Oh!" it exclaimed. "Six hundred and forty years have I walked about the world and I've never seen a brewery of eggshells before. Truly humans are the stupidest creatures if they think that they can eat such a thing!" Then suddenly realizing that it had given itself away it departed like a shadow with a loud whoosh up the chimney to be lost amongst the smoke, *and when the woman looked again, there was her own healthy child sleeping soundly in the crib.*

This basic story, with a number of variations, is told in many parts of the Celtic world, such as Ireland, Scotland, and in the Isle of Man, demonstrating how widespread the belief was.

In Scotland too an infallible means of detecting a changeling was to leave a set of bagpipes by the side of the crib. Because no fairy—no matter how old or sickly—could resist playing a musical instrument, the house would soon be filled with fairy music and the changeling would thus reveal itself.

Usually a "changed" infant never grew up, but died at a fairly young age. In an odd way, perhaps, the belief in changelings provided a measure of comfort for the bereaved parents. After all, it was not really their child who had "died"—their infant was still alive and well somewhere, albeit along with the fairies. There are numerous tales in Scotland, Ireland, and Wales centered around one of these changelings dying, and when the parents came to inspect the crib they found nothing there but an old burned and blackened stick in the place where their so-called child had been. Sometimes it is even a twig or the branch of a tree, symbolizing the fairy's close connection with the natural world.

Some of the "changed" children did survive, although they were often weak and their health was frail. In many cases their wits were not good, to the point of being mentally deficient. Several years ago I was taken to see an alleged changeling living with a family in County Fermanagh in the North of Ireland. This was a boy of 16 who had been "changed" as an infant. Although regarded as mentally deficient and subject to the care of social services, he was still regarded as a fairy changeling by some of the older members of his family, such as his grandparents and great aunts. They were extremely wary, if not rather frightened of him, and always treated him with a kind of deference. These old beliefs still persist in some corners of the world even today.

Stories of changelings also appear in Scandinavian folklore; however, there it is said that trolls carry off young children who are prized for their beauty in troll society. Children with blond hair and blue eyes were especially at risk, because they were particularly valued among the troll-kind and attracted these fairies. Trolls carried children to their underground realm to be raised as slaves. However, according to Scandinavian tradition, a child might be returned if the changeling was brutalized or suffered violence, such as being whipped or beaten, usually with flails. This drove the troll creature away and its kind were then obliged to return the baby they had stolen. Alternatively, the parents might place the infant in an oven, which was slowly heated until the changeling revealed itself and cried out to be set free. In 1860 a Swedish woman was convicted by the courts for killing her deformed son by suffocating him in a heated oven. These were extremely grim ways of detecting a changeling, but in some communities they were sometimes considered necessary.

In Malta, where fairy abductions also seem to have been common in times past, the method for attempting to get the victims back was less severe. The *mibdul* (changed child) was taken to St. Julian's Bay on the northeast coast of the island and placed beneath a statue of the saint that stood there. There it was given a kind of sand bath and was fed on a certain type of cordial, which was made from a secret recipe. This *might* drive the fairy out, but the results were not always guaranteed.

Xana

In the Asturian region of Northern Spain, as late as the 19th and early 20th centuries, small children were believed to be carried away by local fairies known as Xana. The Xana are reputedly invariably female and dwell in caves along the banks of rivers and near pools and waterfalls. They are probably a folklore remnant of old nature spirits and are usually depicted in some tales as beautiful young girls with long, fair hair, and in others as small, dark, almost emaciated creatures. However, they also have children (xaninos), which they cannot properly look after, because their breasts cannot produce milk. In order to have the children suckled, they leave them in the cribs of human children, taking the human occupant in exchange. The human mother will then raise the fairy child as her own until it is weaned, and then the Xana will take it back—but she will not necessarily return the child that she has taken. Indeed, in some tales, the Xana drowns the

stolen infant in the pond or river where she lives as she cannot look after it herself.

If the parent suspects that the child in the crib is not a human one and that there has been Xana activity, then the only way to dispel it is to make it reveal its true age, and this is usually done by some form of trickery. A common story in Northern Spain concerning such stratagems closely resembles *The Brewery of Eggshells* as recounted previously. As soon as the changeling has been exposed, the Xana will be forced to return and restore the baby it has taken.

Patupairehe

Another fairy or spirit (the distinction is often somewhat ambiguous, as we have seen) believed to carry off human children is the patupairehe (also known as the turehu) of New Zealand, who appear in Maori legend. Although more interested in human women (the predominantly male patupairehe are fiercely sexual entities who continually lust after human females), they have been known to seek out and carry off children in order to keep some human females whom they have already abducted. Their sexual prowess is prodigious, and human women whom they have captured and ravished sometimes give birth to creatures that are half human and half fairy, which they cannot really love. In order to retain these women, the patupairehe exchange these halflings for a human child, which they steal from nearby communities, and the human women can look after them. The patupairehe are not all that much different from humans—they are roughly about the same height or slightly smaller, but their skin is much paler than that of Maori, and has a reddish or golden tinge to it. Unlike the Maori they do not wear tattoos or any form of adornment. Their language is completely unintelligible and bears no resemblance to any other tongue. They tend to live in the deep forests of the islands or on the high mist-shrouded mountains, and apart from their voracious lust for human women they tend to shun human contact and thus are seldom seen. The patupairehe are hunters with main hunting grounds reputedly in the Waikato-Wapa Delta Country near Hamilton in North Island and in the Takitimu Mountain Range in Western Southland, but few people there ever see evidence of their passing. However, it is in these areas that most abductions and changelings occur.

If parents suspect that they have a changeling in their crib the baby will look pale and emaciated; there is a certain way of detecting this and a way to get their child back if this does occur. All patupaire-he are pyrophobic—they fear fire or anything to do with it. Therefore, the way to drive away the changeling is to feed it food that has been cooked over an open fire (it is thought that the patupairehe eat their food raw and without benefit of any form of cooking). The changeling will flee and the stolen child will be returned safe and sound.

Adult Abductions

So far we have considered the stealing of very small children by the fairies, but it was not unknown for grown adults to be abducted as well. However, in many of these instances, those who were abducted were often returned after a period of time. And, as with some alleged alien abductions today, some people seem to be more prone to being taken by the fairies. Several years ago I spoke to an old man living near Ballinaleck, in Southwest Fermanagh, Northern Ireland, who spoke of a family of which several members had been abducted by the fairy-kind for certain periods, but each time had come back after several days or weeks. Some of that family had been abducted more than once—the old man referred to one member (a man) who had been abducted no less than seven times. The longest he'd been away from home had been a year, and he had returned home wearing exactly the same clothes as when he had vanished.

The fairies had lured a number of people away by creating "patterns" (fairy shapes) resembling people that they knew or who were dead. In the case of the family mentioned above, the fairies had made shapes of dead relatives in order to draw them away and into the fairy realm.

The use of a "pattern" seems to have been quite a common tactic among the fairies, who used it to tempt many people away with them. In her book *Vision and Beliefs in the West of Ireland* (published in 1920), Lady Augusta Gregory tells of a visit she made to a "fairy doctor" (local healer) named "Old Dernane," who lived on Inishmann in the Aran Islands. He was supposed to be a great healer and had received his powers from a "pattern." One evening when out walking beside a wall on the island, he had seen the "fairy shape" of a girl he had once known walking along the other side of the wall. He said she had a strong connection with the "Others" (the fairy kind) and it was from her that he had received his healing powers. However, he was also afraid that the "pattern" might draw him away from the world of the living and into the fairy domain, for that was the way of such things.

Fetches

In Scotland, too, fairy shapes or "fetches" were also used as a lure for the living. A number of stories from the Western Isles speak of men and women being taken away after following the phantom shapes of people they knew or figures about which they were curious. In South Uist, for example, a man followed the "fetch" of his dead brother (which several other people also claimed to have seen) into what seemed to be a fairy mist and vanished for almost 30 years. This apparently was early in the 1900s, and according to legend (although this is not verified), he turned up again in the late 1920s or early 1930s, not far from where he had disappeared and looking just as young as when he had vanished. However, his wits were totally gone. A similar story comes from Wales where the Tylwyth Teg lured a farmer into a cave near a place called the Raven's Rock in Betws y Coed, and this time he returned after 10 years with his wits awry.

And yet another remarkably similar tale comes from the Isle of Man where a farmer was lured away by the Phynodderree (these are large, bad-tempered shaggy elves of Manx lore who sometimes help farmers but can be just as nasty toward humans if they so choose) with an image of a former sweetheart. They returned him several months later with his wits gone.

The idea that those who have been with the fairies for any length of time may be mentally changed by the experience is also quite a common one. In most tales, those who return are never the same as they were before abduction. The common phrase "away with the fairies," meaning someone who makes wild statements or who behaves oddly, probably arose out of this notion. The idea is that the fairy world is so different from the human world that the abducted individual's perceptions are altered forever, even upon return to the human world. People who returned from the fairy realm (or indeed simply had prolonged contact with the fairies) were often vague and easily distracted, did not focus on simple tasks, and seemed to have their sight fixed on things that nobody else could see. Or perhaps they were moody and withdrawn, preferring to talk to themselves (or unseen entities) rather than other people. Nowadays this may be suggestive of some form of mental condition, but that is only our modern interpretation; in former times this was a sure sign of fairy involvement. Alternatively, prolonged exposure to the fairy world might produce fierce temperaments and violent eccentricities in some people. Rather than sending them mad, the fairies somehow "changed their nature."

Dolly Pentreath

An example of this was the case of the celebrated Dolly Pentreath, a Cornish woman often described as a "half-witch" and who was described by a writer, Daines Barrington, who lived for a time in Cornwall around 1773, as "said to be coming and going from the fairy world as she pleased." Dolly has acquired something of a reputation on two counts. First, she supposedly lived an exceptionally long life for the period (dying at the age of 102), and second, she was supposedly the last native speaker of the Cornish language (she spoke no English). She lived near the harbor of Castle Horneck in Cornwall where she bought and sold fish; according to an account given by a Mr. Blewitt, she was "coarsely spoken and was dirty about her habits and person." According to legends Dolly would disappear from time to time—not for long, but enough to be noticed—and it was alleged that she was "with the fairies," from whom she obtained certain powers. This, it was said, included the power to foretell the future, and some simple forms of healing (although whether she practiced either of these to any great extent is open to question). According to Barrington (who was the brother of Admiral Barrington), Dolly lived in a "mean hut beside a narrow lane" faced by two other houses, and it was from this hut that the fairies came and went—it was alleged that some of them were seen by her neighbors, entering and leaving by the open door in a cloud like a swarm of bees. From time to time, her voice could be heard shouting in the Cornish language (at times when she was drunk she would even come to the door of her hovel to berate passersby), which none of her elderly neighbors could speak; this was taken to be part of her communication with the fairy-kind. Somtimes he hut would stand empty, and it was believed that Dolly was away on her travels in the fairy realm (cynics might argue that she was simply tramping the roads for a time like a beggar). Her contact with the fairies and her alleged visits to their world, however, made her irascible, bad-tempered, and even more foul-mouthed.

Barrington, who met Dolly in 1773, describes her thus: "Dolly Pentreath is short of stature and bends very much with old age, being in her 87th year, so lusty however as to walk hither to Castle Horneck, about 3 miles, in bad weather, in the morning and back again. She is somewhat deaf, but her intellect seemingly not impaired. She has a memory so good that she remembers perfectly well that at Mousehole where she lives, she was sent for by a gentleman, who had a curiosity to hear the Cornish language, and that the innkeeper where the gentleman came from attended them." (The "gentleman" was in fact Barrington, who had met with her earlier.) The mention that Dolly was 87 in 1773 gives something of a lie to the suggestion that she was 102 when she died in 1777—a longevity alleged to arise from her involvement with the fairies. She was probably no more than 90 or 91, which in itself was a good age for the time.

Although Dolly does not appear to have been married, the account of Mr. Blewitt seems to suggest that she had a "base" (illegitimate) child (according to some legends about her this was with a fairy man), although nothing of it is known. Following her death the idea that she was in fact the last Cornish speaker was laid open to question. It is thought that even in 1777, John Nancarrow of Marazion spoke Cornish. (However, it is also known that he was an English speaker as well—the language he mainly used—and so perhaps Dolly was the only speaker who solely used the language.) Like Dolly, he was also regarded as something of a sorcerer, involved with the darker elements of the fairy world.

Dark Fairies

When Dolly died, it is said that swarms of fairies hung about the doorway as though mourning her passing, and that this suggested her strong link to them. She was buried in the churchyard of St. Paul at Penzance with an epitaph written in both Cornish and English by a Mr. Tomson of Truro (who could read and write Cornish—Dolly herself could not write).

Coth Doll Pentreath, cans ha Deau,
Marow ha kledyz ed Paul plea:
Na ed Egloz, gan poble braz,
Bes ed Egkoz-hay coth Dolly es.

(Old Doll Pentreath, one hundred aged and two,
Deceased and buried in Paul parish too
Not in the Church with people great and high,
But in the Churchyard doth old Dolly lie.)

At least part of Dolly's alleged fairy involvement (and perhaps that of John Nancarrow) arose from her being able to speak a language that few could understand. It was said that Cornish was the language that, being the embodiments of the Cornish countryside, the fairies themselves used. This idea was coupled with her disappearances from home when she was believed to have been away in the fairy realm. There is little doubt that she was a larger-than-life character, and had an explosive temper; this ferocious temperament was put down to having been with the fairies, who were not always regarded as either good or benign. Her alleged age of 102 (which has even been placed on her tombstone) was also attributed to the fairies, who had rewarded her "bad behavior" with longevity. But it was clearly her colorful character and eccentricity that marked her as slightly different from her neighbors, and was attributed to her fairy connections.

Mrs. Sheridan

A similar Irish "fairy woman" was the mysterious "Mrs. Sheridan," whom Lady Gregory met in County Sligo at the end of the 19th century. It is not clear that Sheridan was her real name, even though that is how Lady Gregory refers to her. She had been "away" with the fairies several times—whether against her will or not is also unclear—but from them she had received certain gifts. For example, although poorly sighted, she was still able to "see" the fairies as they came and went through the human world, and what they were up to. She was also considered to be a great healer, even as great as the famous Biddy Early from Clare who had relationships with the fairies and had also allegedly been "taken" by them. Early is often considered to be Ireland's greatest wise woman.

Describing this "fairy woman," Lady Gregory writes:

> *Mrs. Sheridan as I call her was wrinkled and half-blind and had gone barefoot through her lifetime. She was old for she had once met Raftery the Gaelic poet at a dance and had died well before the Famine of '47. She must have been comely then for he said to her "Well planed you are; the carpenter who planed you knew his trade." To which Mrs. Sheridan replied, "Better than you know yours" for his fiddle had one or two broken strings.*

The fairies had taken her at the old ruined castle of Ballinamantane just below her house and took her to a grand ball or dance they were holding. She described a fairy bridge there across a nearby river, which they had built up "in a minute" (the bridge was not usually there), which they tried to get her to cross. At first she would not, but in the end—after the bridge had been raised and lowered several times—she did. Perhaps this act symbolizes her crossing into the fairy world. When there she had been granted many gifts, such as the gift of prophesy and the power to see fairies on a regular basis, but her temperament seems to have changed, and, according to stories, she had a certain "vagueness" about her.

What became of Mrs. Sheridan is unknown—the main account of her comes from Lady Gregory's book, but there are also several old stories—perhaps she was eventually carried off by the fairies, never to return. This was the way of it in some instances.

Anne Jeffreys

One of the most famous of those who came and went with the fairies was Anne Jeffreys from St. Treath (a tiny village near Camelford) in Cornwall. Anne was born in December 1626 into the large family of a poor laborer who couldn't really look after her, and so she was "farmed out" (as was the custom) to the nearby Martyn family. She was a strange, listless girl, who seemed to become even stranger as time went on. She had few friends and seemed to do very little work about the house, preferring to sit in dreamy contemplation for long periods. From time to time she would disappear and return, claiming she had been "drawn away" by the fairies that thronged invisibly in the Martyn's garden, and which only she could see. At first these abductions seem to have been against her will, but later she came to look forward to her "disappearances."

Most of what we know about Anne Jeffreys comes from an account of her life published in a document by Moses Pitt of London. Pitt was a publisher who had heard stories about Anne's queer life and abilities, and he asked his nephew, who was a lawyer, to interview her. At the time of her interview, Anne had been unjustly imprisoned by the notorious Cornish magistrate John Tregagle, himself the subject of much folklore, especially concerning pacts with the Devil. Pitt's nephew did not interview Anne personally, but sent his brother-in-law Humphrey Martin to speak to her instead. Martin reported that Anne was extremely reluctant to speak about her contact with the fairies or about her sojourns in the fairy world, or even about any supernatural powers that she might have acquired as a result of her visits there. At the time of the interview (September 1691), Anne was about 60 years old and was in rather frail and uncertain health. She was also married to William Warren, who was a local herdsman. Any information that she did give about the fairies was given rather unwillingly, stating that she was afraid that people might "make books or ballads of it," which was contrary to fairy wishes. Moreover, the interview was conducted with her just after her release from the infamous Bodmin Gaol, where Anne felt that she had been incarcerated unjustly; she was terrified that, by speaking too frankly about the fairies, she would be arrested once more if her words ended up in print. As a result, her accounts of the fairies and their motives with regard to the human world were extremely sketchy and lacked any sort of detail. Moses Pitt was not satisfied.

Two years later, in 1693, he wrote to Martin again, asking him to attempt another interview, and shortly afterward received word that Anne had been seen again on January 31st. Her mind was wandering and her accounts made little sense—she seemed more concerned that many of the people that she'd known in St. Treath were now dead except one, Thomas Christopher, a blind man. Her accounts were extremely garbled and more vague than before. Martin was forced to be content with collecting some local folklore and stories about Anne rather than conducting an in-depth interview.

From what he could gather, Anne's stay with the Martyn family had been a reasonably happy one. When she had first come to stay with them she had been a healthy and sturdy teenager, if a little bit dreamy and introverted. There was a lot of work around the household and it was sometimes difficult to get Anne to participate in it and help out. She preferred to sit in front of the window, lost in her own thoughts— indeed some people said that she already had the "fairy disposition." When she was 19 she suddenly became aware of small people coming and going near the house, which nobody else in the household could see, and shortly afterward she briefly disappeared, returning after a day or so. From then on she seemed to be aware of about six small beings, all dressed in green, close to the house, watching her intently from the opposite hedge and talking animatedly among themselves. She told the Martyns about it, but they thought that she might be suffering from a fever and put her to bed. Shortly afterward, she disappeared again, returning to the house a couple of days later. Once again she was put to bed to rest, but it often seemed that when those looking after her had gone out, something came into the room. A couple of times the Martyns stepped into the room and found Anne sitting up in bed, soaked in sweat and pointing to the window. "They have just gone out the window!" she cried. "Did you not see them?" However, nobody could see anything, either in the room or in the garden beyond.

Dark Fairies

The sightings and disappearances seemed to be taking a toll on Anne's health, which seemed to be deteriorating as the years went by. She had now become a shadow of her former hearty self. By April 1646, she was often so weak that she "could barely stand upright on her feet" and had become "even as a changeling." She would walk around the various rooms of the house by holding onto chairs and the edges of tables and would often fall into fits. The Martyns were afraid that she might even die from one of these. Indeed, they believed that she was becoming more and more like the fairies with whom she said she went from time to time. Gradually Anne began to recover and was actually able to go to the parish church of St. Teath to thank God for her deliverance and renounce the fairy kind. Even so she was becoming something of a terror to the other members of the household, who feared her fairy involvement and her suspected fairy powers. Her strange behavior was putting an intolerable strain on the Martyn family.

One evening when everybody was out of the house in the fields for the harvesting, Mrs. Martyn desired to get flour from a local mill, but she was afraid of leaving Anne alone in the house, for she might bring in the fairies and set fire to it. So she persuaded Anne to come out of the house and sit in the garden—then she locked her out whilst she went to the mill. If the fairies were to take her now, then let them—perhaps it would be a blessing.

On her way to the mill, Mrs, Martyn stumbled on a patch of uneven ground, badly twisting her ankle as she fell. Unable to get up again, she was found by a passing horseman who lifted her onto his steed and brought her back home in great distress. When the reapers arrived home again, the pain in Mrs. Martyn's leg had not eased and a servant was dispatched to fetch Dr. Lobb, a local surgeon from Bodmin, to see to her. After he had gone, promising to return, Anne came in from the garden and without prompting gave the entire circumstances of the accident, even though she had not been about when Mrs. Martyn was brought home and she had spoken to nobody. She also asked to see the injured leg. Taking it upon her lap, she proceeded to stroke it very gently, asking Mrs. Martyn if this gave her any ease. The good woman had to admit that it did. At this Anne admitted that it was "a gift" that she had been given by her sojourn in the fairy world, and indeed so soothing was her touch that Mrs. Martyn called a servant and sent him to tell the doctor not to return, as she had "no need of him." Anne then amended her explanation concerning "the gift" by stating that it was sanctioned by God and his angels to give succour to the unfortunate, and once again Mrs. Martyn believed her.

When the two women were alone in the room (the serving man having withdrawn), Anne confined to Mrs. Martyn how she had come to be involved with the fairies. She said that she often took illnesses and faints, and that these were caused by fairies who lived in the hedge opposite the house and who were seeking ways to communicate with the people there. These sicknesses often left her weak and light-headed for many days. From time to time she imagined herself carried away by the small people (for such she described the fairies to be) to some sort of realm that lay beyond mortal view. She did not disclose anything about this place except to say that it was "wondrous." However, there was a hint of menace in her description. When Anne had been shut out of the house, the fairies had appeared and had asked her if she been locked out against her will. When she replied that she had, they became extremely angry and had declared that Mrs. Martyn would not fare well because of her actions. At that very instant, Mrs. Martyn had fallen on the uneven road, badly injuring herself. Mrs. Martyn, it was suggested, should take this as a warning not to upset Anne in any way again. It was a threat, which her guardian took very seriously.

The story of Mrs. Martyn's leg, together with more tales (most of them fanciful) about Anne and the fairies spread like wildfire through the countryside, and people with all manner of illnesses and injuries from all over Cornwall and beyond came to see her to see if she could help them. She had the "fairy gift," after all. They came from as far away as Lands End and from parts of England, and even some from as far as Scotland, just to see her. And all sorts of people came—from the very old to young babies, all seeking her aid. Anne helped some of them, and others she said that she could not, for the "fairies would not allow it." Sometimes people arrived only to be told that Anne was gone, having been taken away into the fairy realm, either voluntarily or involuntarily. However, she always returned. After the incident with Mrs. Martyn, Anne suddenly ceased to eat. The only time she appeared to break her self-imposed fast was on Christmas Day when she ate beef with the family. On Christmas Day she said the fairies had no power over her, and she could do what she pleased. She was also able to tell the Martyns when someone was coming to the house, even long before they actually appeared—this she claimed was another "gift," which she had acquired in the fairy world, and which she could maintain as long as she did not eat.

There were, however, inconsistencies in Anne's story. One of the sons of the house had occasionally gone up to speak with her, but found the door to her bedroom locked. There appeared to be a great deal of activity on the other side of the door, so he knocked loudly. Anne's voice came from inside the room saying, "Have a little patience and I will let you in presently." Dropping to his knees, the boy squinted through the keyhole and saw Anne munching her way through a heap of food, which she had presumably hidden away in some secret place in the room. When she had finished she appeared to stand up and give thanks before opening the door. She told the boy that she had been "communing with the fairies," and that they had not allowed her to open the door and let him see them. Later she was challenged about the food and she changed her story and declared that this was "supernatural food," which the fairies had brought her from their world and, although a search was made of the room at her insistence, no trace of her feast was found.

And, as if to reinforce her supernatural claims, another incident occurred shortly afterward. A neighbor had called to see Anne about some matter and went straight up to her room to speak with her. The bedroom was completely empty, even though Mrs. Martyn had insisted that she was there. The neighbor searched high and low, but found no trace of her. But as he turned to go back downstairs again, Anne walked out of the bedroom behind him. She said she had been away in the fairy realm, later amending the story to having been in the room all the time, but invisible to human eyes (this, she claimed, was another "gift" that the fairies had given her). It was, however, suggested that Anne might have somehow hidden herself somewhere close by and made it "appear" that she had returned from the fairy realm—an allegation that she vehemently denied.

Shortly afterward, Anne gave an astonished Mrs. Martyn a beautiful silver cup, which held about a quart of liquid. She said that she had brought it back from the fairy realm; at this revelation the woman became so alarmed that she refused to have anything to do with it, for fear it might be enchanted. The cup mysteriously disappeared, just as mysteriously as it had appeared. However, the story drew much unwelcome attention to Anne, and it was even suggested that the cup might have been stolen from somewhere else.

The incident of the cup drew the attention of local ministers and magistrates in Anne's direction. The magistrates had been aware of her alleged powers for some time, and were extremely wary of them; together with several ministers they paid Anne a visit in order to question her. They cited fear and suspicion in the region as their sole interest for doing so, but it is also clear that they wanted to expose her as a fraud, a madwoman, or a heretic. They questioned her rigorously. What was the fairy world like? Anne refused to say, because she claimed she had been forbidden by the fairies to disclose anything concerning their world. What did the fairies say to her when she met with them? She might not have remembered because the fairies had magically erased their words from her mind. Were the fairies in fact agents of the Devil? Anne didn't really know, but she did not think so. She proved evasive, but when points were put directly to her, she was able to argue against them and with seeming conviction. A local priest was brought to her to try to convince her that she was actually consorting with Infernal Spirits and was in danger of damning her immortal soul. Anne listened gravely, but said nothing. When the ministers had left she turned to Mrs. Martyn (who had been with her throughout the questioning) and said, "They call now." Lifting a large Bible that the Martyns kept in the house, she went outside into the garden. When Mrs. Martyn went out after her, there was no sign of Anne, though it's quite possible that she might have been hiding nearby. She was gone for a number of hours, returning with the book, saying that she had been in the fairy realm.

Dark Fairies

The fairies, she warned, were extremely angry that Anne had allowed herself to be interviewed by ministers and that the Martyns had been complicit in this. They were furious that the priest had declared that they were Infernal Spirits and cited The First Epistle of John: Chapter 4, Verse 1: "Dearly beloved, believe not every spirit, but try the spirits whether they be of God."

Her "reading" of this text was of particular interest to those around her, because Anne was supposedly illiterate. She continued to practice her cures and foretellings and to meet with the fairies near the Martyns' house.

The ministers and magistrates, however, hadn't given up their interest in her. At last John Tregeagle, a Justice of the Peace, issued a warrant for Anne's arrest on suspicion of witchcraft, and had her confined in the notorious Bodmin Gaol, regarded as a hellhole. She was kept there for a very long time (although it is now impossible to say for how long, as the Gaol records have long been destroyed). According to legend, Anne foresaw the constables' coming with her eye of prophesy. She pleaded with the fairies to hide in their realm but they refused her. With the case fixed against her, Anne was sent to prison. During her trial, it appeared that she continued not to eat, although it was thought that the Martyns secretly smuggled her food when they visited, for they had profited financially from Anne's alleged "powers."

She languished in Gaol for some time. At one stage John Tregeagle had her removed from prison and brought to his own house where he deliberately starved her in order to see if the stories about her receiving "fairy food" were true. Some others said that the fairies visited her in prison and brought her food, but suspected that any sustenance was secretly brought by well-wishers who came to see her.

In the end, she was released in a considerably weakened state, but was not allowed to return to the Martyn household. The magistrates suspected that the family had been complicit in her fairy activities in some way. Instead, she was sent to live with a Mrs. Frances Tom, Mr. Martyn's sister, a widow living near Padstow. She continued to be secretive, although whether the fairies came to visit or take her back to their own country is unknown. It is thought that she sometimes foretold the future and continued to do the occasional healing. But such activities were always carried on in secret, as the magistrates were still watching her. At some point later in her life Anne got married, although in keeping with her now reclusive lifestyle absolutely nothing is known about her husband except his name, William Warren. She does not appear to have lived with him, nor does she appear to have had many dealings with him after their marriage, even going so far as to retain her maiden name of Jeffreys (a rather scandalous thing to do in those times). It is also not certain as to when she died.

What are we to make of Anne Jeffreys? Was she simply a poor and deluded girl who believed she was in communication with fairies living close by her house? Was she a scheming and manipulative individual who, in collusion with the Martyns, contrived to make herself known as a purported seeress and healer for financial gain? And if so, did she make up aspects of the "fairy relationship" in order to promote herself? Or was she in effect a practitioner of diabolic arts and in consort with dark and infernal spirits as the clergy had alleged? And why was she arrested and detained for so long, and then not allowed to return to her former home when released?

At least part of the answer to that last question perhaps was found in some manuscripts discovered in the Bodleian Library in Oxford in the 1930s by the author and scholar Hamilton Jenkins that seem to relate directly to Anne. They are in the form of letters dated February and April 1647:

> I can acquaint you with "news" of a young girle which foretells things to come, the most have fallen true. She eats nothing but sweetmeats, as Alemans [almonds] comfited and the like, which are brought to her by small people dressed in green, and sometimes by birds. She cures most diseases, the Falling Sickness (epilepsy), especially broken bones only with the touch of her hands. She hath been examined by three able Divines and gives a good accompt of her religion and hath the Scriptures very perfectly, though quite unlearned. They are

fearful to meddle with her for she tells them to their faces that they are unable to hurt her. At present she is in Bodmin, at the Mayor's house. She says that the King shall enjoy his own and be revenged on his enemies.

In that last sentence, which had supposedly come from the fairies, Anne had condemned herself and shown that her fairy companions were willing to enter into and comment upon human politics. These letters were written after the main conflict of the English Civil War when the vanquished King Charles I was captured. However, in 1647 when he was still a prisoner, Charles was secretly negotiating with the Scots, who planned to invade England on his behalf on the promise that England would become Presbyterian (a promise that the King had no intention of keeping). In the end the full-scale invasion never took place (though there were skirmishes), as the Scots realized they could not trust Charles, but England was in turmoil because nobody knew whether the king would actually return to the throne. Anne's comment that the king would "enjoy his own" was therefore loaded with political significance. Charles would be turned over to the Parliamentary forces and publicly executed as a common criminal at Tyburn in London by the Parliamentary Government in January 1649. After his death, Anne's (and the fairy) pronouncement became even more politically charged.

This was the time of the Republican Government when Parliament (not a King) ruled the country. Charles I, however, had two sons, Charles and James, both of whom fled to France, and many people in England still harboured a return to the Monarchy. They looked to his son Charles (later Charles II) to return and drive the Parliamentarians out in France and Holland; the heir to the throne seemed to be gathering an army to do just that. Anne's utterances therefore smacked of treason against the ruling authority. She was, in fact, quite fortunate that she was not executed herself, given the unsettled, almost paranoid climate of the times. The words did, however, give the notorious witch-persecutor John Tregeagle enough ammunition to have her arrested and confined to Bodmin Gaol. This would also probably explain Anne's reluctance to speak to the publisher's agent in later years. She must have finished her days as a frail and secretive woman, a condition directly due to her alleged association with the fairy-kind. Whether she had been "carried away" by them or whether she had actively sought out their company is still a matter that is open to question.

Reverend Kirk

Very different in both style and temperament from the dreamy and secretive Anne Jeffreys was another individual who claimed to have been carried away by the fairies—the Reverend Robert Kirk, minister of Old Kirk and Aberfoyle in Scotland. Kirk's substantial essay (often described as a book) *The Secret Commonwealth of Elves Fauns and Fairies*, completed and circulated in 1691 (but not published until 1815 by Longman and Co.) created something of an uproar when it first appeared, and brought a great deal of criticism on a man who was described as "The Fairy Minister."

Robert Kirk was born in the Manse at Aberfoyle around 1641 (the exact date is sometimes disputed). He was the seventh and youngest son of the Reverend James Kirk who had long been installed as the Episcopalian Minister there. His gender and position in the family are significant. Scottish folklore (and some other folklore besides) has long held that a seventh son might possess special powers—the seventh son of a seventh son is invariably regarded as having the gift of prophesy and healing. Robert seems to have been slightly "different" from other children. There was no doubt he had a prodigious intellect and he was rather "solitary"—not in the vague, dreamy way of Anne Jeffreys—but simply preferring his own company. He would go for long walks in the Aberfoyle countryside visiting old earthworks and fairy hills in the district. It was almost as if he was drawn to them. Writing in a foreword to a modern edition of *The Secret Commonwealth,* a distant descendant, R.B. Cunningham-Graham, makes the suggestion that he may have been a changeling left by the fairies. This, of course, is simply poetic license, but perhaps was mentioned at the time.

The country around Aberfoyle would later be strongly associated with the Highland outlaw and hero Rob Roy McGregor, but at the time of Kirk's childhood it was more associated with fairies and supernatural entities. There was one area that was particularly linked with the Good People, a spot known as Doon Hill, and when he would return to Aberfoyle as a minister, Kirk would still walk up to this fairy-haunted place as part of his daily exercise. It was there that he was supposed to meet with the fairy kind.

The manse he was born into was a dual-language household, meaning that both English and Gaelic were in common usage. Indeed, Robert Kirk was a fluent Gaelic speaker in later years and actually translated the Bible from English into Scots Gaelic (this is still known as "Kirk's Bible" in some parts of Scotland). There has also been a suggestion that Kirk could also speak Erse, which is sometimes counted as a pre-Gaelic language (though this is open to question), and which was spoken in both the Scottish Highlands and the North of Ireland; it was claimed he had learned the language from the fairies. However, if the language existed as a separate tongue, it had more or less died out by the seventh or eighth centuries with the fall of Irish Dalriada (a kingdom that spanned both Western Scotland and the northerly tip of Ireland), or else, more probably, it had merged into Gaelic. The name was also used to refer to Scots Gaelic itself.

There is no doubt that Kirk was an intelligent individual. Although his family was poor, he was still able to go to the high school in Dundee and then to Edinburgh, graduating with an MA in 1661. He then obtained a Bursary from the Presbytery of Dunblane, which enabled him to graduate with a Doctor of Divinity, aged 20, in 1664 (one of the youngest such doctors in Scotland at the time). He married twice—first in 1670 to Isobel Campbell, daughter of Sir Colin Campbell of Mochaster, with whom he had two children. When she died in 1680 he subsequently married a daughter of Campbell of Fordy, with whom he had one son; he later became a minister at Dornoch.

In 1669 (some say 1664) Kirk was appointed as Minister of Balquihidder near Stirling where he would serve until 1685. In Balquihidder Glen there were several fairy "knows" (small hills), which were strongly associated with the Good People, and Kirk seemed to make a daily pilgrimage to these places, "commune with Nature," as he said. Local people believed that the fairies had either lured him there or else he had gone to speak with them in an attempt to gain special powers. When at St. Andrews he had been impressed by tales of the Reverend Robert Blair—a northern Protestant Divine and a former minister there—who could cure the disease of scrofula or King's Evil with a wave of his hand. Blair had a great reputation all over Scotland because of his miraculous feats—some of which are undoubtedly exaggeration. It is said he wished to acquire powers, hence his journeys to the fairy hills in the Balquihidder Glen.

His first wife died and was buried in the local church at Balquihidder, while Kirk would remain there as minister for another five years before returning to Aberfoyle to take over as minister. Once again he resumed his daily walks into the country mainly to fairy-haunted Doon Hill to meet and converse with the Good People. It was out of these alleged meetings that the *Secret Commonwealth* emerged, originally published as a tract in 1691, purportedly giving a description of the fairies, their land, and their ways.

The latter half of the 17th century was a time of great religious turmoil in Scotland. The English monarchs had tried to impose the rule of Anglican Bishops on the Scottish people, though they resisted in the zeal of Presbyterian reform. Many churches were becoming stricter in outlook and reaching to crush old beliefs that still existed in the Highlands and in the West. Fairies rapidly became equated with witches and with infernal spirits, and so with *The Secret Commonwealth* Kirk was in some ways stepping outside his role as minister. And to some, this was how it was perceived. This was a time when religious dogma and attitudes were becoming extremely fixed and religious and social tolerance was low. It was a time when witchcraft allegations flourished all over the country—some concerned with social issues and others with religious differences. Catholics and Anglicans were particularly associated with the Dark Arts, and notions of the "old ways" were regarded with suspicion. Kirk seemed to support the ancient traditions in his pamphlet, as if in opposition to strict Church teaching, and became known as "the Fairy Minister"—a man of whom many people were wary. His theory was that fairy beliefs were not incompatible with Christian teaching and that good Christians might consort with the fairy-kind.

Dark Fairies

On May 14th, 1692, Kirk took his customary walk up to Doon Hill, but did not return; he was later found dead on the summit of the hill. After his death it was said that the Fairy Minister had actually departed into the fairy realm and that the thing that was found on Doon Hill was nothing more than a "stock" (or unliving representation) of him. Kirk, it was said, was watching events around Aberfoyle from fairyland.

This belief seemed to be borne out by a story that circulated widely after his death. A relative, the Reverend Patrick Graham, recounted how, shortly after his body had been found, Kirk's spirit appeared to another relative, Graham of Duchray, to tell him that he was not really dead. He had fallen in a swoon on Doon Hill, and his spirit had been carried off by the fairies and was now trapped within their realm. The coffin that had been laid to rest in the "Old Church" at Aberfoyle contained only stones. His wife was now ready to give birth to another child, which the spirit prophesied would be a boy (as indeed the child was). At the baptism of this posthumous child, Kirk's spirit would reappear in the church, and if Graham would throw a knife over it, Kirk would be freed and would return to the world of the living. According to tradition, Kirk's spectre did indeed appear at the baptism, but Graham was so taken aback and terrified that he failed to throw the knife, and the spirit left the church by another door. Presumably, it was trapped within the other realm. Some traditions say that it is trapped in a tree on the Hill itself—a tree that is still known as "The Minister's Pine." The book that he left behind has seen several reprints since 1815, and is now regarded as a classic of fairy lore, despite the controversy that surround it when it first appeared.

Besides being very different in temperament from Anne Jeffreys, and apart from being the author of a controversial pamphlet on fairies, the story of Robert Kirk, "the fairy minister," introduces another element to fairy abductions: those who were abducted were still alive and held in fairyland or some other realm (perhaps against their will) and might be released if certain actions were undertaken. They might appear as spirits (as indeed did Kirk) giving details of how they might be released, or else local folklore might suggest how such release might be achieved.

Although both Anne Jeffreys and Robert Kirk were 17th-century figures and very much characters of their time, this notion was still current in 19th-century Ireland and appears in the case of Bridget Cleary in South Tipperary at the turn of the 20th century. The occurrence in 1894 became widely known as "The Clonmel Witch Burning," and is generally regarded as the last "witch burning" in the British Isles.

Witch Burnings

The case itself and the subsequent trial for the murder of Bridget's husband Michael Cleary is a rather complex one, which involves the subtle undercurrents of local tensions and hostilities that existed in the Clonmel and Fethard areas of South Tipperary. Much has been written about it, and several radio and television programs have been made about it, each seeking to give some sort of perspective on what actually happened and the reasons for it. Although it is not proposed to consider all the local disputes and family problems that may have contributed to the event, the involvement of the fairies remains very high.

And of course, the Clonmel Witch Burning has to be set against the background of fairy changelings, which was an extremely prevalent belief in parts of Ireland, even during the 19th century. Indeed, even well into the 20th century many "fairy doctors" (men and women) existed in Ireland, each with the power to detect a changeling, whether child or adult, in the local population where they lived. Many of the methods that they used have been detailed already—placing children on shovels, pouring foxglove potions down their throats, and so on—the most efficacious being plunging a suspected individual into cold, running water or confronting him or her with fire.

Many of these "remedies" were carried out at various times all over Ireland, mainly directed at those who were too weak or too confused to offer much resistance. In County Kerry, for example, the *Morning Post* reported the following account from the Tralee Assizes in July 1826:

> *Ann Roche, an old woman of very advanced age, was indict-*
> *ed for the murder of Michael Leahy, a young child, by drowning*
> *him in the [River] Flesk. This case turned out to be a homicide*
> *committed under the delusion of the grossest superstition.*
> *The child, though four years old, could neither stand, walk, [n]*
> *or speak—it was thought to be fairy struck....*
>
> *Upon cross-examination, the witness said that it was not*
> *done with intent to kill the child, but to cure it—to put the*
> *fairy out of it.*
>
> *Verdict: Not guilty.*

This astonishing account was recorded by Irish folklorist Thomas Crofton Croker in 1829. It was, however, not the only such incident of its kind. On May 19, 1884, the *Daily Telegraph* reported another case from County Tipperary, which bears disturbing similarities to the Kerry case:

> *Ellen Cushion and Anastasia Rourke were arrested at Clon-*
> *mel on Saturday charged with ill-treating a child three years old,*
> *named Phillip Dillon. The prisoners were taken before the May-*
> *or when evidence was given that the boy, who had not the use*
> *of his limbs, was a changeling, left by the fairies in exchange for*
> *their original child. While the mother was absent, the prison-*
> *ers entered her house and placed the lad on a hot shovel under*
> *the impression that this would break the charm. The poor little*
> *thing was severely burned and is in a precarious condition. The*
> *prisoners, on being remanded, were hooted by an indignant*
> *crowd. But we must regard it rather as a protest against the*
> *prisoners' inhumanity than against their superstition.*

The account, quoted from Edwin Sidney Harland's *The Science of Fairy Tales* serves to demonstrate how deeply the belief ran in Irish, and Celtic society. There are also similar stories from all over Scotland and Wales of invalid children being placed in hot ovens or suspended over fires on meat hooks in order to "drive the fairy from them." In certain circumstances, the suspected changeling might even be dismembered as a way of returning it to the supernatural realm. On January 30, 1888, for instance, Joanna Doyle appeared at Killarney Assizes on a charge of child murder. The defendant was 45 year of age, of wild appearance, and could speak practically no English—only Gaelic. She was charged with butchering her mentally retarded son Patsy with a hatchet, in which she had been aided by her husband and three other children. She insisted that 13-year-old Patsy was not her child at all, but "a fairy and a Devil." Another child, Denis, described as "an imbecile" was also considered to be under threat. She was placed in the Killarney Asylum where she proved to be a violent patient. Her 18-year-old daughter Mary commented: "I heard people say he [Patsy] was a fairy and I believed them." There were similar grisly incidents around the end of the 19th and beginning of the 20th centuries in Roscrea, North Tipperary, and in County Armagh.

The most famous of all the changeling cases, however, was that of Bridget Cleary from Ballyvadlea, near Clonmel, South Tipperary, in 1895, which made headlines far beyond Irish shores. It drew interest from English thinkers such as E.F. Benson (author of the famous "Mapp and Lucia" books), who wrote an article concerning it in the learned journal *The Nineteenth Century* in June 1895.

Before considering the actual case, it is necessary to make one other point. In the cases of adult fairy abduction, it was generally believed that the fairies left behind a "stock"—an animated representation of the person whom they had abducted. This behaved and acted very much like the abducted person, but in reality, the "stock" had no will of its own and was controlled by the fairies. It was through such creatures that the malignant fairy kind could exercise their will and might spread evil through a community. It was vital, therefore, that such "stocks" be detected and eliminated as soon as possible, for who knew what danger they might bring to a locality? This was central to the case of Bridget Cleary.

Bridget Cleary

Bridget Cleary died near the place where she had been born—in Ballyvadlea, not far from Clonmel, South Tipperary. When she died in 1895, she was 26 years old, and according to descriptions of her in the

Dark Fairies

Cork Examiner, she was a pretty woman, of medium height, and with a strong personality. She was well known in her home area—though she was widely known as Bridget Boland (her maiden name)—by laboring folk and gentry alike. Many remarks had been passed by local men of all levels of social status about her good looks. As a girl she lived with her father Patrick and Bridget Boland who were local, laboring people and largely unremarkable in their ways. They were Roman Catholic and deeply superstitious.

Indeed, superstition—particularly concerning the fairies—was very much a part of the area in which she grew up. From where she lived, people could see the distant slopes of fairy-haunted Slievenamon, the legendary mountain stronghold of the Fenian Knights, and allegedly the abode of many supernatural creatures. Between it and Fethard town, many "slieveens" dwelt. These were "fairy doctors" and "cunning men" who specialized in the ways of the fairies (although the term has now come to mean "trickster"). There were men such as Denis Ganey, who lived in a thatched cabin at Kyleatlea on the mountain's lower slopes, and John (Jack) Dunne, a limping and toothless man who tramped the streets of Clonmel and Fethard, regaling anyone who would buy him a drink with stories of fairies and ghosts. Such men knew of "haunted" sites throughout the region, particularly around Slievenamon itself. Nearer to the Bolands' house, however, lay the brooding bulk of Kylenagranagh Hill, which had just as sinister a reputation as the fairy-haunted mountain. It was topped with a fairy fort or rath (since demolished) which was a place of dread—where the Sidhe Court (very much like the Unseelie Court) frequently met to plot evil against humans. Local people mostly avoided going near the place.

Despite being what might be termed "a modern girl," Bridget felt little need to move away from this environment. She was outgoing and forward-thinking in her ways—she was the first person in the district to have a new Singer sewing machine (a real sign of modernity) on which she made her own clothes and some for her neighbors. She was now a fairly prosperous young lady and could have had her pick of most of the young men around Ballyvadlea. It came as a surprise to everybody when she picked the dour and sullen Michael Cleary as a husband.

They had met in Clonmel where Bridget was working as an apprentice dressmaker and Michael was working as a cooper. They were an extremely odd match—she a lively young girl and he a dark, brooding man. Even so they were married in August 1887 when Michael was 27 and Bridget was 18. For Bridget, it was a young age for marrying (most women did not marry until they were roughly 26). The marriage was also an unusual one—Michael continued to live and work in Clonmel while Bridget returned home to live with her parents near Ballyvadlea Bridge. To be fair she may have been looking after her mother who was unwell.

In the late 1880s, Michael and Bridget Cleary, together with Bridget's parents, applied to the Cashel Poor Law Guardians for the tenancy of a new cottage that had been built in the townland of Tullowcaussan, which was about half a mile from Ballyvadlea Bridge. The cottage was a relatively modern and tidy one with uninterrupted views of Slievenamon, but it had one unfortunate aspect—it had been built on the site of a fairy rath. The Guardians had taken no account of local superstitions and had completely destroyed the old fort on which the cottage now stood, much against the will of people. The Clearys were unsuccessful in their application and the cottage went to another laborer. The local fairies, however, did not appear to take to this man and kept him awake every night with their unearthly screeches until at last he relinquished his tenancy and fled the area. The Clearys were offered the cottage and moved in.

They were surrounded by friends and relations. Patrick Boland's widowed sister Mary Kennedy, for example, lived a short distance away at Ballyvadlea Bridge. Her sons Patrick, James, and William were all laborers and lived with her, together with her granddaughter, Katie Burke, who was her daughter Johanna's eldest child. Johanna, with her husband Michael Burke, and several other children, lived less than a mile away. The two girls were quite close—in fact, when Johanna had married in August 1884, her bridesmaid had been her cousin Bridget Boland. At the time of Bridget's death Johanna (or "Han" as she was known in the locality) would have been about 34. Bridget was therefore well supported by those whom she knew in her new home.

Bridget settled in well and became something of a local businesswoman. Besides a dressmaking business, she kept a few hens, selling the eggs to neighbors (this was very common amongst Irish women as it gave them an independent source of income).

The winter of 1894/95 was a particularly severe one in South Tipperary. Farm work was delayed, and with no employment for the laborers many even faced destitution. There was heavy snow, and for a long time roads were impassable, with hardship everywhere. The air was extremely sharp and cold. Things didn't pick up again until March 1895.

On Monday, March 4, 1895, Bridget Cleary walked from her house across Ballyvadlea Bridge to the squalid cabin beside Kylenagranagh Hill where Jack Dunne lived with his wife Kate, in order to collect money for eggs. Although the day was sunny it was fiercely cold. It had been snowing the night before and the top of distant Slievenamon glistened white. Dunne cabin seemed empty and nobody answered her persistent knocking. Jack and Kate Dunne had no children and spent much of their time drinking in the pubs of Clonmel and Fethard, leaving their home abandoned for long periods. As she stood on the doorstep, Bridget felt a peculiar chill, which she credited to the terrible cold of the day. She walked home quickly to "get to the fire," but in spite of the heat the chill did not go away.

The next day, it still hadn't left her, and she was also complaining of a violent headache. Her family was slightly concerned and great attention was paid to the place where she'd first noticed the chill. It had been on Jack Dunne's doorstep near Kylenagranagh Hill. The place was badly fairy-haunted and Dunne was widely regarded as a "fairy man." In fact, he complained of a pain in his back, which he had received after being attacked by fairies who had lifted him out of his bed and had thrown him in the yard. Some people wondered whether there was a connection to dark fairy magic.

As the days passed Bridget's condition slowly got worse. It was as though she had contracted pneumonia out of the chill and she was put to bed, only allowed up to sit at the fire for brief periods. She had become a pale shadow of a healthy, vibrant young lady. Hearing of her illness, Jack Dunne called to see her as she sat up in bed one afternoon. The room was dark and the old man's eyesight wasn't good. Peering around the door, he drew back slightly.

"That's not Bridget Boland!" he whispered. Coming from the lips of somebody else that might have been taken as a general comment, but coming from a "fairy man" it had a particular significance. Jack Dunne had an extensive knowledge of the fairies, and coupled with the rumors that were circulating about the origin of Bridget's chill his words took on a profoundly sinister meaning. It might mean that Bridget had been abducted by the fairies of Kylenagranagh Hill and that the creature in the bed was no more than a "stock," which had been left in her place. And it suited some people to think this, for while Bridget was reasonably popular in the area she also had a number of enemies who probably thought that she was too "high and mighty." There was also the gossip that after almost 10 years of marriage, the Clearys had no children, perhaps a sign of "fairy blight." Everybody had remarked on how the once vital woman had deteriorated into a shivering invalid who couldn't even leave the house. Dunne was asked to look more closely at her.

One of the ways in which fairy involvement might be detected was to measure the legs of an individual. Those who had been molested or changed by the fairies usually had one leg shorter than the other—indeed this was the case with Jack Dunne. While Dunne was measuring Bridget, Michael Cleary arrived home. Moodily he listened to what the fairy man said before pronouncing "She is not my wife at all, but a fairy-thing from Kylenagranagh Hill." Even so, he did nothing.

By Saturday, March 9, Bridget's condition had grown much worse and it was thought that she had received a fresh chill. Despite Jack Dunne's alleged powers, the family was determined to put their faith in a medical doctor. Patrick Boland walked the four miles to Fethard to get Dr. William Crean to come to see his daughter, stopping at the house of one of the Poor Law Guardians in order to obtain the "red ticket," which entitled her to free medical attention. However, Crean didn't come. It was a bad weekend, rainy with a strong wind blowing—the roads up into Ballyvadlea were muddy and covered with tree debris, and perhaps the doctor didn't fancy venturing into such an isolated area; maybe he had medical business elsewhere. There were stories that Dr. Crean was a little too "fond of the drink," and that he attended to his duties in a rather haphazard fashion. He still hadn't come by Monday, so Michael Cleary walked to Fethard to fetch him. Still he didn't come, and all the while Bridget's condition worsened. Johanna Burke said that she was running a high fever and was barely strong enough to stand. On Wednesday, March 13, Michael Cleary walked into Fetherd again, but he also sent to nearby Drangen for the parish priest, Father Cornelius Ryan, to come and attend his wife. This did the trick, for on Wednesday afternoon Dr. Crean called at the Cleary house. He diagnosed "nervous excitement and a slight bronchitis," prescribed a medicine, and went back to Fethard. Later in court he would reveal that Bridget Cleary had been attending him for six months, but he would not say why. It was thought that she had contracted tuberculosis and had been attending a TB clinic in Clonmel.

Slowly, pent-up difficulties in the relationship between Michael and his wife began to emerge, as recounted by Johanna Burke at Cleary's trial. The sick woman told her cousin that there had been animosity between Michael Cleary and his mother-in-law who had been regarded by many as a "fairy woman" in the style of Jack Dunne, with a knowledge of fairies and herbs. She told Han Burke that Michael believed that on her death, her mother had somehow passed on to her Bridget all her arcane knowledge—"He's making a fairy of me," she whispered. There seemed little doubt that Michael Cleary was nervous of his invalid wife. Much of the time, he stood by his doorway looking toward distant Slievenamon, and when he did speak much of his talk was about Denis Ganey, the "fairy doctor" who lived at Kyleatlea on its lower slopes. On March 14 he actually set out to "speak with Ganey over the mountain" about his wife.

Denis Ganey was a middle-aged man with a prematurely grey beard streaked with yellow. Similar to Jack Dunne, one of his legs was shorter than the other—a sure sign of the fairy connection. Nobody knows what passed between him and Michael Cleary in his reasonably neat cabin at Kyleatlea, but Cleary arrived home with a potion from the fairy man, which he said held "nine cures." The potion probably contained lusmore (foxglove), which was supposed "to burn the entrails out of any unearthly thing," including fairies. The conversation with Ganey had convinced Michael Cleary that his wife was a fairy and he returned home in a confused and excited state. He mixed the potion with the "beestings" (the first milk of the day drawn from a cow) and proceeded to offer it to Bridget.

Later that evening a crowd of friends and neighbors—the Burkes and the Simpsons—came to the house. As they approached the building they could hear a man's voice shouting, "Take that you rap!" The door was locked and some of them tried to look in the window, but the wooden shutters were drawn and they could see nothing. They knocked on the door, but from inside Michael Cleary called out that nobody should come in yet. Then they heard snippets of a heated conversation: "Take it you old bitch." Then, to everyone's surprise, the door flew open and a man's voice called "Away she go! Away she go!" Michael Cleary came to the doorway, bathed in sweat, and invited his neighbors in. They looked at him strangely, but he explained that he had kept the door closed, as the house had been full of fairies.

One of the first through the door was Johanna Burke, and she later described a scene of brutal horror. Patrick Boland was sitting in the lamplit kitchen, but everyone else was in the bedroom. Bridget was lying on the bed, with Jack Dunne (who was not a sturdy man) holding down her head by the ears. Her cousin Patrick Kennedy was at the far side gripping her right arm and his brother James her left. The younger brother William lay across her legs to prevent her from moving or trying to get up. They were trying to force her to take something on a spoon from a small black saucepan. Cleary put his hand over her mouth to prevent it from coming back up again because, it was said, if it fell on the ground, Bridget could not be brought back from the fairies. He kept asking her "Are you Bridget Cleary or Bridget Boland, the wife of Michael Cleary in the Name of God?" She answered him three times before he was satisfied. He forced at least some of Ganey's mixture down her throat while the neighbors were there. When it was done all the men present clapped their hands and shouted, "Away with you! Come home Bridget Boland in the Name of God!" They slapped her about the face and chest. One of those present noticed some burn marks across the invalid's forehead and was later told that she'd been threatened with a red-hot poker in order to make her take the herbs. Hearing the voices of the visitors in the kitchen, Bridget screamed loudly for help. Jack Dunne, however, had other ideas.

"Make good the fire," he said. "And we will make her answer." Lifting Bridget from the bed, Jack Dunne at her head, James Kennedy her feet, and Michael Cleary following with the spoon and saucepan they carried her to the fire, which was now burning brightly. According to Johanna Burke, Bridget was conscious and well aware of what was happening. Without too much trouble, they held her over the steadily burning flames. With desperation edging his voice Patrick Boland asked: "Are you the daughter of Patrick Boland, the wife of Michael Cleary?" "I am Dada," Bridget answered. The men held her there for at least 10 minutes before taking her back to bed. Perhaps they felt temporarily convinced that they had driven the fairy creature out.

About 7 a.m. on Friday, March 15, Father Cornelius Ryan was called from the parochial house at Drangan to visit Bridget. He had actually called on her two days before, as requested, and was told that she was dying. He had given her the Last Rites of the Church. Now Michael Cleary turned up once more and asked him to come again; somewhat reluctantly, Father Ryan did so. He arrived at the house about 8 a.m. and gave Bridget Holy Communion, but, according to her cousin Johanna, she did not swallow the Host, and later removed it from her mouth using her fingers—something expressly forbidden by Catholic teaching. This was to prevent it from falling into the hands of witches and fairies who desired the sacred wafer for their own occult purposes. Before he left Father Ryan asked Michael Cleary if Bridget was taking the prescribed medicine, and her husband replied that she wasn't, as he had no faith in it. The priest seemed to concur and spoke of William Crean as being "always drunk."

In the afternoon, an argument of some kind seems to have developed between Michael Cleary and Johanna Burke over payment for some milk, which the former alleged she sold to Bridget. The invalid seems to have given her cousin the shilling she owed, but before she did, she put it under the blankets of her bed and rubbed it on her leg as if putting a pishrogue (spell) on it. The allegation may have arisen

because Johanna had an underlying jealousy of Bridget, but it fired up her husband even more.

Some more visitors called that night and Bridget was dressed and brought to the fire while Johanna Burke made some "stirabout" (porridge). One of the neighbors, Tome Smith, asked how she was feeling and she replied that she was "middling," but that her husband was "making a fairy of her." She also told him that Michael wouldn't let her drink any of the milk that she'd bought from Johanna Burke—it might be enchanted. After some of the neighbors had left tea was made and Bridget was given three pieces of bread and jam. As she came to eat the third piece, Michael jumped forward and forced it down her throat. "Swallow it! Is it down?" he shouted. He then struck her across the face, flinging her to the cottage floor. "Oh Han, Han!" she called to her cousin in desperation. Still in a fit, Michel Cleary tore off his wife's clothing, leaving her in her chemise in front of the men and, taking a burning stick from the fire, he tried to ram it down her throat. Then, taking the house key, he walked across and turned it in the lock, effectively locking everyone in the cottage.

At this point most of the people, clearly terrified, fled into the next room. They could hear Bridget shouting, "Give me a chance!" and then heard her head strike the floor, followed by her scream. In the bedroom Mary Kennedy heard her son William cry out, "Mother! Mother! Bridgie is burned!" She rose up and both she and Johanna Burke rushed to the door, but found their way blocked by Michael Cleary. "What ails ye?" shouted Mary Kennedy. Michael looked at her solemnly. "I believe she's dead," he said. Then, walking over to the window, he took down the lamp and, unscrewing a cap, poured paraffin all over the prone body on the floor. There was no doubt that he was now out of control and as he attempted to set fire to Bridget, he was stopped by Mrs. Kennedy, whom he pushed away.

"What are you doing with the creature?" cried the old woman as she reeled back. "Is it roasting her you are?" Michael Cleary suddenly darted forward and set fire to his wife's paraffin-soaked body, which was ablaze in an instant.

"For the love of God, Michael!" shouted James Kennedy, coming out of the adjoining bedroom and seeing what was going on. "Don't burn your wife!" Half-turning, Michael Cleary looked at him blankly. "She's not my wife," he answered in a low, flat voice. "She's an old deceiver sent in place of my wife. She's been deceiving me for the last seven or eight days and deceived the priest today too, but she won't deceive me any more. As I began with her, I will finish it with her. You'll see her go up the chimney." By this he referred to the traditional escape route of the fairy changeling.

Seeing that the man's wits were clearly gone, William Kennedy asked him for the house key so that he might go, but Cleary drew a knife and told him that he would "run him through" if he attempted to leave; at this the boy fainted clean away. Patrick Boland then came out and told him that if there was anything he could do to save his daughter, then he would do it. Cleary answered him that he could bury Bridget next to her mother, who had also been "of the fairy." He further told Patrick that next Sunday if he (Cleary) would go to Kylenagranagh Fort, the real Bridget would come riding to him on a white horse; if he could cut the golden straps that bound her to the animal, she would be free and his once more. This is what "Ganey over the mountain" had told him, although he would later declare that Bridget had told him that. Then in a sudden change of mood he warned the rest of the family, "If you come out any more, I'll roast you as well as her." Everyone withdrew into a bedroom, leaving Cleary alone with his wife's body. Still holding the lamp, he unscrewed the cap again and poured paraffin on her three more times before sitting down to watch the flames burn the body. Seeing someone peep out of the bedroom he shouted: "You're a dirty set! You'd rather have her with the fairies in Kylenagranagh than have her here with me!"

Later, and under duress, Patrick Kennedy went with Michael Cleary to bury the body in a "secret spot" nearby while the rest of the family remained locked in the house. Once the body had been buried, Cleary made all who had witnessed the atrocity kneel down and swear on the Holy Name not to reveal it to a soul. They should simply tell those who asked that Bridget had "gone away."

The next Saturday, March 16, Jack Dunne, who was in a badly agitated state, accompanied Michael Cleary and Michael Kennedy to Drangen village in order to attend confession in the chapel there. It was the curate, Father McGrath, and not Father Ryan, who heard confession that day. Dunne went into the confessional first and the curate sent him out, asking Michael Cleary to come in and see him. Cleary went in weeping, and spoke to Father McGrath, although what was said remains under the seal of the Confessional. The curate, however, determined that he was in "no fit state to receive communion" and sent for Father Ryan, who was in the Parochial House. The three men talked for a long time; all the while Michael Kennedy remained outside in the chapel yard. Eventually Father Ryan emerged and walked straight across the road and into Drangen Police Barracks to speak to Acting Sergeant Patrick Egan.

What passed between the two men has never been disclosed, but it was enough to arouse police suspicions. Egan was well known in the locality and had probably heard about the disappearance of Cleary's wife. He had also probably heard the stories circulating about Cleary's behavior and about the fairy connection. However, he couldn't investigate without a formal complaint being lodged. Taking another policeman with him, Egan walked home with Michael Cleary, asking questions as he walked. Cleary apparently stuck to his story that Bridget had left, and said he didn't know where she had gone. As he left the house, Egan claimed he heard a distressed Patrick Boland call from inside: "My daughter will come back to me!" The old man would insist right up to the trial that Bridget was alive and well and living "elsewhere" with the fairies.

Egan was suspicious and asked for some policemen from Clonmel to be sent to Ballyvadlea to help look for Bridget. As they arrived, a formal complaint against Michael Cleary was made. Unusually, the name of the complainant has never been disclosed, but it was widely thought to be a neighbor named William Simpson. Simpson, a Protestant, was a married man, but was long suspected of having had an affair with Bridget while Michael was working in Clonmel. Simpson claimed that Michael Cleary had approached him for the loan of a revolver that Simpson was known to possess so that he could go up to Kylenaghranagh Fort and "bring back his wife." Simpson didn't lend him the gun, but later claimed to have seen Cleary going up to the hill with a large table knife. Allegedly, Cleary had waited there for a long time for Bridget to appear on a white horse, but had seen nothing. Simpson also claimed to have seen Bridget ill-treated in her home the previous Thursday night. He made these allegations in a sworn statement in front of the local magistrate, W. Walker Tennant, Justice of the Peace.

By now the situation was becoming too complex for the police in Drangan village to handle, and Patrick Egan passed the case to Inspector Joseph Wansborough in Carrick-on-Suir, who ordered a full-scale search of the area near the Cleary's cottage. Police were soon searching the areas of Dragan, Clooneen, and Mullinahone, whereas Wansborough visited a number of homes in Ballyvadela, taking copious notes from those whom he interviewed. Johanna Burke also swore a statement in front of the magistrate saying that Bridget Clearly had left home while ill and had "disappeared." Tennant now asked Wansborough to bring charges, and, given all the concrete information that he now had, it is surprising that the first person the Inspector arrested was Denis Ganey, a man who had never even met Bridget Cleary.

On Friday, March 22, 1895, officers from the Royal Irish Constabulary, guided by William Simpson, searched an area of boggy ground in Tullowcrossaun, near the Cleary home. Away in a corner of a field about a quarter of a mile from the cottage, Sergeant Patrick Rogers of the Mullinahone Constabulary noticed some freshly turned earth and crushed bushes. Constables Somers and O'Callaghan helped him to dig down about 18 inches where they found a dirty sheet wrapped round what looked like a woman's body. The corpse had been pulled up into what looked like a crouching position with the knees near the chin, and the body was badly burnt. It was naked except for a few remnants of clothing, all of which were badly charred and had burned into the skin, and a pair of black stockings. The head was covered in a sack and was largely untouched. There was still a gold earring in one of the ears. Tearing away the sacking, Rogers looked at the face and identified it. They had found what remained of Bridget Cleary.

Now that the body had been found, arrests followed quickly. Police arrested Michael Cleary, Patrick Boland, Mary Kennedy, Johanna Burke, the Kennedy brothers, and Jack Dunne. All across Ireland and far beyond, interest was suddenly focused on the remote corner of

Dark Fairies

County Tipperary. Ballyvadlea became known around the world as a place of dark superstition and sinister events.

The case came to trial at the Summer Assizes in Clonmel on July 4, 1895, under Mr. Justice O'Brien. He paid scant attention to the talk of fairies and "witchcraft," but all the same such stories still persisted and were seized on by the press. The folklore and rumor had no effect on Michael Cleary's final sentence—he received 20 years penal servitude for the manslaughter of his wife while in a disturbed state.

Jack Dunne and the Kennedy brothers (who had assisted in forcing Ganey's poison down Bridget's throat) were found guilty of "wounding"—Patrick Kennedy was sentenced to five years imprisonment. Jack Dunne was sentenced to three; the other two were sentenced to one year each. Patrick Boland and Michael Kennedy received six months, but Mary Kennedy was set free by order of the court. There was some speculation that she had given information that had helped convict the others, but this is far from certain. By contrast, her daughter Johanna Burke revoked the first statement that she had given and had turned Queen's evidence; in the trail she became the chief witness for the prosecution, and the evidence she provided was crucial.

From the Assizes at Clonmel the prisoners were taken to Mountjoy Prison. Jack Dunne was released on licence and returned to Ballyvadlea. His wife Kate had died and he finished his days as a labouring man, broken and unwilling to talk about the incident. The Kennedys too were released on licence and returned home to work as laborers, refusing to say anything. Michael Cleary, however, remained in prison, being shifted between Mountjoy in Dublin and Maryborough (now Portlaois) Prison in County Laois. According to some accounts, he learned to work as a tailor, but was always a quiet and withdrawn inmate. He was released on licence from Maryborough on April 28, 1910. He may have returned briefly to County Tipperary, but it is certain that in June that same year he boarded a ship bound for Montreal and vanished from the pages of recorded history. It is possible that in Canada he changed his name and disappeared.

The fairies of Kylenagranagh had taken their final revenge. One of the more sinister legacies of that time lies in an odd rhyme that local children still sing as they play their skipping games:

Away With the Fairies

Are you a witch, or are you a fairy,
Are you the wife of Michael Cleary?

The idea of the fairy abduction and of the changeling has often underpinned significant parts of both the folklore and the individual human tragedies of English, Scottish, and Irish cultures, as well as those of many others. But what do they mean? Did such abductions and changes actually take place? Were those who vanished simply spirited away, perhaps by members of some other species who found difficulty in breeding and who needed new blood to ensure their survival or was it all, as perhaps in the mind of Michael Cleary, simply a delusion? We may never know but, perhaps, even in the 21st century, it is still advisable to keep our children close by.

Come away O human child,
To the waters and the wild.
—*The Stolen Child*, W.B. Yeats

Conclusion

The Other Sort

erceived relations between humans and fairies have always been difficult. At least part of this difficulty may emerge from the conflicting ideas humans hold about what fairies actually *are*. The image that many hold of tiny humanoid figures flittering along on gossamer wings or of jolly sprites sitting under hedges are, of course, the sanitized visions of mainly English Victorians who, confronted by tales of vicious, violent, spiteful, and even blood-drinking creatures felt that they could not pass such fables on to succeeding generations (particularly their children) in that form. This is the image that has been expanded and developed through the 1950s and 1960s by children's writers such as England's Enid Blyton until they have become part of our overall perceptions. The original "fairies," as we have seen, were something very different. They were possibly the remnants of Aboriginal races that strove to hide away from Mankind in the mountains and the forests; they were memories of ancient and often barbaric gods and spirits whom earliest men had worshipped, or they were the embodiment of our ancestors' deepest fears as they ventured into what were unknown regions, which served as an explanation for the disasters that befell them there. In the eyes of the Church and other organized religions, they were the agents of Satan, or at the very least the evil that had once stalked the land. Nor were they particularly well disposed toward our ancestors—the idea of a kindly fairy helping out a distressed human is something of a myth. Indeed, in many cases, they were feared and avoided if possible.

As time went on, fairies often took on more and more attributes and characteristics. They began, for instance, to develop personalities, something that made them appear more like humans, although that personality was often malicious and hostile toward Humankind. We have already mentioned fairy bands such as the Sluagh attacking individuals by hurling stones or rocks at them as they passed, or even sometimes carrying them away, we've detailed the Unseelie Court, plotting mischief and danger against those who lived in the areas where the court might meet. We have already noted that it was believed that some fairies might even drink blood or draw the strength and good from individuals themselves—as did the fairies in the remote Kerry mountain stronghold mentioned by Sean O' Suilleabhain. This ideal is embodied in entities such as the Leannan Shee—the fairy lover or fairy mistress—who drains the strength from those who make love to her, eventually leaving them a wasted husk. However, she also has the power to inspire great song or great poetry in the individual with whom she chooses to mate, and in fact is said to have been the partner of some of the great Gaelic bards and poets of ancient Ireland. This makes her something akin to a muse, but she is also a vampire, physically wasting those whom she courts. In many respects, she is an embodiment of the arts themselves—full of beauty and wonder—but in their worst sense, ultimately destructive. Perhaps such imagery (the embodiment of the artistic endeavor) is how the Leannan Shee was initially perceived.

Also sometimes driven by malicious or evil intent are the Abbey Lubbers of medieval Saxon folklore and who were to be found in many parts of England. These are often malignant imps who inhabit the cellars and vaults of ruined abbeys (hence the name) or abandoned houses. They were vicious entities, attacking travelers who passed by their abode by hurling stones and rubbish at them and sometime injuring them. Not only this, but they placed concealed obstacles in the roadway, causing passersby to trip, fall, and often injure themselves. These beings were never actually seen, but usually behaved much the same as the shadows, which had gathered around the ruined buildings where they lived. No reason was usually given for such behavior, except that they despised and hated humans. In some tales, however, it was said that they guarded treasures, perhaps left by monks, and sought to keep humans from finding it. Although in certain stories the Abbey Lubbers appear to be friendly, it is their malignant side that always seemed to come to the fore in most folklore. And, according to traditional tales, many other fairies behaved in a similar fashion.

All these ideas were added to a central fairy belief and became a part of fairy lore. They also added to the reputation of the fairy people

and usually defined their character—wary, malicious, and quick to violence. Fairies were therefore beings to be feared, if received wisdom was to be believed. They were (in Irish parlance) "the other crowd," who lived away from Mankind in secret places, and were best to be avoided by all decent humans. Fairies were devious and cheating. In many Irish tales it was unwise even to answer a direct question from a fairy creature, because that answer would place the individual within the fairy's power. When their paths crossed, fairies were continually asking humans questions in order to try to ensnare their immortal souls. Such a belief underpins this old folktale from the Tyrone/South Derry border area in the North of Ireland. It was told by the great Tyrone storyteller George Barnet.

I heard my mother tell this story often. There was a girl lived near her in a place called Lavey, which was where my mother came from. A big strong girl she was too, very healthy. Every evening it was the custom for her and her sister to go to the woods and bring in the cattle for milking. To get to the woods, they had to cross a big field, which was supposed to be badly fairy-haunted. This evening they were on their way to the wood and her sister was walking a little way ahead of her. A fairy stepped out from behind a bush and said, "Would ye like a tune on the fiddle?" And she not being one to talk to a fairy walked on, looking straight in front of her. And a fairy stepped out from behind a tree and asked, "Would ye like a tune on the fife?" And the sweat was standing on her head, but she walked on. And a fairy stepped out from behind a big standing stone and asked, "Would ye like a tune on the bodhran?" She then fainted and her sister came back and lifted her and carried her home. She was never the same after that and instead of being a big strapping girl, she was thin and sickly and never very well. And she couldn't stay around Lavey because she was continually polluted by fairies. In the end, I think she went to America.

Even being directly addressed by a fairy, it would seem, was injurious to one's health and welfare. And if speaking to a fairy was dangerous, accepting fairy money was to damn one's immortal soul. In any case fairy money never actually remained *as* money, as has been noted in the story *The Trip to London* recounted earlier in the book. It has the tendency to revert to less salubrious things—leaves, acorns, pebbles, and cow or sheep manure. Even monies that might have been given kindly by fairies (such as by the Macara Shee as part of their largesse as they trooped through the countryside, or in exchange for some service) were extremely damning, said the Church, and the acceptance of them would inevitably consign the individual soul to Hell.

Certainly across the Western European countryside—and in some other parts of the world as well—fairies were often viewed at worst as malicious and vindictive creatures, and at best indifferent, usually condescending beings that held a deep-seated contempt for human, whom they were believed to consider as inferior to themselves. They were, in fact, a race apart. Whether this meant, as we have suggested, a physically different race (and there have been some archaeological and anthropological excavations—the most recent being in 2008 on the island of Flores in Indonesia—which have showed that there were indeed extremely small humanoid species existing in prehistoric times) or whether these were simply the "humanization" of early powerful gods whom our ancestors worshipped, is open to question. It may be that fairies were simply a recognizable embodiment of the rampant forces of nature that could, at any time, overwhelm the puny human communities who often regarded them with fear and awe. Whatever they were, Mankind was wary of them, and usually, as we have seen, portrayed them in myriad forms and with varying powers, many of which were used in inimical ways toward humans.

Indeed, there are so many variations of the fairy kind and their powers that it has proved impossible to cover them all. And because of the ethos of the book, we have only mainly concentrated on those fairies who have posed a threat or who have shown overt hostility toward Humankind, omitting those whose motives might be considered to be less problematic. Fairy creatures such as gnomes (or kaukis in Prussia where they are said to have originated), although rather unpleasant to look at, are said to be extremely benevolent and helpful toward both human and animals (indeed, in some areas they do housework that humans cannot be bothered to do). And pixies, although certainly mischievous entities, are not generally considered to be immensely hostile toward Humankind in strict folkloric terms.

Today, most of our ideas about fairies come from the stories we were told when we were young, or from television or films. In fact, many adults often tend to regard fairy stories as the sole province of children. Consequently they appear as good-hearted, diminutive versions of ourselves with perhaps added supernatural powers, which they use only for the benefit of the humans they encounter. They often appear in popular imagery as small female entities flitting through a remote forest glade on gossamer wings, or some wise or playful little man sitting beneath a hedge or on a toadstool (regarded in some parts of Europe as fairy seats), unwilling to do passing humans any harm. Much of these are sanitized Victorian impressions, and, as we have seen, are almost the total reverse of the strict folkloric motif. Fairies usually sought to at best inconvenience and at worst injure their human neighbors; they stole or blighted their livestock and their crops, and they caused them misfortune whenever they could. Fairies were not benevolent beings to be sought out by children, no matter what the stories say; they were dark and sinister entities who were to be strenuously avoided. The image that many hold today is totally erroneous.

However they may appear, fairies will always be with us in some shape or form. Ideas concerning "other folk" who may share the countryside with us have existed since earliest times, and although their images of them may have changed throughout the years, they still form a significant part of our cultural psyche. And it is highly likely that they will continue to create both interest and appeal in the future with the release of such franchises as *Wings,* featuring Disney's latest star, Miley Cyrus, which will ensure that the topic will remain highly popular and at the forefront of our consciousness.

Fairies, it seems, are and always have been everywhere. They are skulking in the shadows and lurking in the dark places not all that far from our homes. They may be in the bushes or in the trees that you

Dark Fairies

can see from your window they may be just beyond the furthest street lamp as you close the door for the night. Be very careful, for they may not be what you think they are! They may have lulled you into a false sense of security about them. They seem to be friendly, childish things! But our ancestors knew that the truth was different and now, so do you. Look under a bush or hedgerow if you hear a strange sound coming from there. What you see there may amaze and probably terrify you!

Bibliography

Bottrell, William. *Traditions and Hearthside Stories of West Cornwall*. Private printing, 1870–1880.

Briggs, Katherine. *The Fairies in Tradition and Literature*. New York: Routlege and Kegan Paul, 2002.

Campbell, John G. *The Gaelic Otherworld*. Edinburgh: Berlinn, 2005.

Cooper, Joe. *The Case of the Cottingley Fairies*. London: Robert Hale Publishers, 1990.

Curran, Bob. *Creatures of Celtic Myth*. London: Cassell Books, 2000.

———. *The Dark Spirit*. London: Cassell Books, 2001.

———. *A Field Guide to Irish Fairies*. Mankato, Minn.: Appletree Press, 1996.

———. *The Truth About the Leprechaun*. Dublin: Wolfhound Press, 2000.

Curtin, Jeremiah. *Irish Folk Tales Collected 1935–1906*. Dublin: Talbot Press, 1960.

Curtiss. J.P. *Visions and Apparitions*. British Columbia: New Society Press, 1980.

Cohn, Norman. *Europe's Inner Demons*. New York: Macmillan, 1975.

Conan-Doyle, Arthur. *The Coming of the Fairies*. London: Hodder Press, 1922.

Dark Fairies

Dann, Penny. *The Secret Fairy Handbook*. Tewkesbury: Orchard Press, 1997.

Dasent, G.W. *A Collection of Popular Tales from the Norse and North German*. London: Norroena Society, 1906.

Delarue, Paul. *The Borzoi Book of French Folk Tales*. New York: Alfred Kopf, 1956.

Douglas, George. *Scottish Fairy and other Folk Tales*. London: Scott Publishing Co., 1901.

Evans Wentz, W. *The Fairy Faith in Celtic Countries*. London: Oxford University Press. 1911.

Fielder, Leslie. *Freaks: Myths and Images of the Secret Self*. New York: Simon & Schuster, 1978.

Gardner, Edward L. *A Book of Real Fairies: The Cottingley Photographs and Their Sequel*. London: Theosophical Publishing House, 1945.

Gill, W.W. *A Manx Scrapbook*. London: Arrowsmith, 1932.

Graves, Robert. *Fairies and Fusiliers*. London: William Heineman, 1917.

Gregory, Lady Augusta. *Visions and Beliefs in the West of Ireland*. London: Colin Smythe Ltd. Book Publishers, 1976.

Grimm Bothers. *Grimm's Fairy Tales*. Oxford, UK: Routledge, 1947.

Haining, Peter. *The Leprechaun's Kingdom*. London: The Slaney Press, 1979.

Hartland, E.S. *Science of Fairy Tales*. London: Scott Publishing, 2008.

Henderson, George. *Survivals in Belief Among the Celts*. London: McLehose Publishing, 1911.

Hodson, Geoffrey. *Fairies at Work and Play*. London: Theosophical Publishing House, 1925.

Kirk, Robert. *The Secret Commonwealth of Elves, Fauns and Fairies*. Mineola, N.Y.: Dover Press, 2008.

MacDonald, George. *Dealings With the Fairies*. London: Murdock Publishing Company, 1867.

McGregor, A.A. *The Peat Fire's Flame*. Edinburgh: Ettrick Forest Press, 1937.

Mackenzie, Donald. *Scottish Folk-Lore and Folk-Life*. London: Blackie Books, 1935.

McNeill, Marion. *The Silver Bough*. New York: MacMillan Books, 1957.

McPherson, J.M. *Primitive Beliefs in the North-East of Scotland*.

London: Longman's Press, 1929.

Pourrat, Henri. *A Treasury of French Tales*. Sydney, Australia: Allen & Unwin, 1953.

Purkiss, Diane. *Troublesome Things*. New York: The Penguin Press, 2000.

Sendak, Maurice. *Where the Wild Things Are*. New York: Harper and Row,1962.

Simpkins, J.E. *Country Folklore*. London: Folklore Society,1914.

Simpson, E.B. *Folklore in Lowland Scotland*. London: Letchworth Press, 1908.

Simpson, Jacqueline, and Jennifer Westwood. *Lore of the Land*. New York: Penguin Books, 2005.

Southern, Edmund. *That Monstrous Shape: Supernatural Beings in Other Lands*. London: John Prentiss & Sons, 1897.

Starr-Johns, Cecil. *The Fairies Annual*. London: John Lane, 1918.

Taylor, J.E. *The Fairy Ring: A New Collection of Popular Tales*. London: Murray & Co.,1846.

Thomas, Keith. *Religion and the Decline of Magic*. New York: Penguin Books, 1971.

Dark Fairies

Wallace-Dunlop, M., and M. Rivett-Carnac. *Fairies, Elves and Glower-Babies*. London: Duckworth Press,1899.

Wright, E.M. *Rustic Speech and Folk-Lore*. London: Oxford University Press, 1913.

Yeats, W.B. *The Celtic Twilight*. New York: Colin Smythe, 1994.

Index

Abbey Lubbers, 177
aboriginal
     race, 30, 34
     species, 43
Adam and Eve, 30
Adam Kadmon, 40-41, 43, 65
Aiobhaill, 50-51
alfar, 30, 32
Amadan-na-Briona, 45-48
angels, 62-63
Anufat, 111
askaluiker, 34
bald hills, the, 119
banshees, 17, 49-52
barguest, 14, 16

Baron Hylton, 14-16
birth among the fairies, 128
black elves, 97
Blavatsky, Madam H.P., 24, 44
bogeymen, 108
Boland, Bridget, *see* Cleary, Bridget
Boru, Brian, 50
brollaghan, 68-70
brownies, 120
changelings, 20, 129-138, 146, 153, 157-159, 169
Cherokee folklore, 93, 117-118, 120
cherubim, 63, 65
Cleary, Bridget, 159-172

Dark Fairies

Clonmel Witch Burning, the, 157
Coltha, 49
Conan Doyle, Sir Arthur, 25-28
Cottingley fairies, 24-28
Creek Indians, 121-122
demons, 20, 66
Disney, Walt, 6, 21
djinn, 66-68
draugr, 99
dryads, 28
duende, 108-110
dwarves, 33, 35, 92, 96-99
Eddas, the, 33
elf houses, 32
elfbolts, 101
elfshot, 97
elves, 6, 33, 97-98
Faerie Queen, the, 10
fairies and the dead, 36
fairy blight, 163
Fairy
    Cavalcade, the, 44, 54, 70
    Godmother, 7
    Minister, the, 155-156
fairy
    courts, 84
    crosses, 119
    food, 14
    fort, 61
    funerals, 81-83
    music, 124
    rath, 161
    shapes, 138-139
    wind, 80-81
fallen angels, 12
Far Liath, 69-70

Fatui, 7
Fear Gorta, 48-49
Fenian Knights, 160
fetches, 139
Fir Bolgs, 41
Fool of the Forth, 45-48
fox spirits, 115
Germanic lore, 106
giants, 35
gluggagaegir, 34
gnomes, 36, 92, 180
goblin, 117
goblins, 6, 92, 99, 101-106
Good Folk, the, 19
Good People, the, 154-155
Greek mythology, 28-29
Grey Man, the, 69-70
grogochs, 38
Gryla, 34
Hell-Ride, the, 84
hiisi, 105-106
Hildaland, 37
hobgoblin, 108
house elf, 16
huldufolk, 30, 32-37, 100
huli jing, 115-117
Hy Brasail, 13
Hylton Castle, 15-16
Jacob's ladder, 65
Jeffreys, Anne, 144-153, 157
Judaculla, 118
Kadmon, Adam, 40-41, 43, 65
kallikantzaroi, 106-109
kappas, 114-115
karakoncolos, 108
keening, 52

King Arthur, 8, 14
Kirk's Bible, 154
knockers, 100-101
kobolds, 55, 92-101, 123
Lady Gregory, 45, 50, 138, 143
Leannan Shee, 177
LeFay, Morgan, 8
leprechauns, 6, 40, 53-55, 95, 120
Lovecraft, H.P., 44, 83
Macara Shee, 44, 70, 105, 180
Maori legend, 137
meliae, 29
mibdul, 135
Milesians, 42-43
moon-eyed people, 122-123
Morgan LeFay, 8
mounds and raths, 68
mounds and tumuli, 101
Mrs. Sheridan, 142-143
Muqarribun, 68
Nacht Ruprecht, 103
Norse tradition, 97-98
nunnehi, 55, 117-123
Pagan
        gods, 11-12
        spirits, 20
        times, 52
patupairehe, 137-138
Pentreath, Dolly, 140-142
Phynodderree, 139
prehistoric races, 12
proto-races, 49
Queen of Elfland, 10
rath, 77, 160
Reverend Kirk, 153-157

Santa Claus, 103
Scandinavian folklore, 100, 106, 134-135
Scottish folklore, 153
seraphim, 63, 65
Sidhe Court, the, 160
Sluagh, the, 70-86, 89, 97, 101, 176
Sluagh-na-Marbh, 81
Tam Lin, 8-11
taotaomonas, 110-112
Tata duende, 109-110
Tinkerbell, 6
tomtin, 103, 106
tree fairies, 28
trolls, 34-36, 38, 99-101, 105, 110, 134
Tuatha de Danann, 12-13, 41-44, 47, 49, 51
tumuli and mounds, 49
Tylwyth Teg, 60, 128, 139
Ugulu, 118
Unseelie Court, the, 84, 86-89, 92, 160, 176
vampires, 99, 102-103, 107, 116, 177
vitterfolk, 35
Wadi Rum, 67-68
Washer at the Ford, the, 49
witchcraft, 150
Witches' Sabbat, a, 84
World Tree, the, 106-107
Xana, 135, 137
Yeats, W.B., 44-45, 105
yokai, 112, 114
Yunwi Tsusdi, 123

About the Author

Dr. Bob Curran was born in a remote area of County Down, Northern Ireland. The area in which he grew up was rich in folklore—especially the folklore of the supernatural—and this gave him an ear for and an interest in the tales and beliefs of many people. He worked a number of jobs before going to university, where he received a doctorate in child psychology. Even so, his interest in folklore and folk culture was still very much to the fore, and this prompted him to write a number of books on the subject, including *Celtic Lord and Legend*; *Vampires*; *Werewolves*; *Zombies*; and *Lost Lands, Forgotten Realms*. Having taken a degree in history, he now lectures and broadcasts on matters of historical interest, and acts as advisor to a number of influential cultural bodies in Northern Ireland. Most recently he has been working on advisory bodies regarding cultural links between Northern Ireland and the West of Scotland. He currently lives in Northern Ireland with his wife and young family.